GEORGE
WASHINGTON
IN THE
FRENCH &
INDIAN WAR

GEORGE WASHINGTON
IN THE
FRENCH &
INDIAN WAR

Scott C. Patchan

THE
History
PRESS

Published by The History Press
Charleston, SC
www.historypress.com

First published 2024

Manufactured in the United States

ISBN 9781467149754

Library of Congress Control Number: 2023945831

This book is dedicated to the memory of my father,
Raymond J. Patchan, U.S. Army.

CONTENTS

PREFACE

Fort Necessity National Battlefield is the first historic site that this author visited in his life. During a visit to my grandparents' house near Uniontown, Pennsylvania, my father took us to visit Fort Necessity when I was six years old. I distinctly remember walking a trace of Braddock's Road, visiting the general's grave, touring the reconstructed fort and aiming the swivel guns; most vividly, I recall the musket firing demonstration by a British soldier. The highlight of the visit occurred when he allowed me to place my hand on the stock of the rifle while my father snapped a photo. This visit proved to be the first of many to military history sites across the United States and fostered a lifelong passion.

I would like to also extend appreciation to several people who made this book possible. First and foremost, my acquisition editor at The History Press, Kate Jenkins, has been the model of patience in this effort and a source of encouragement throughout the process. John Maass of the National Museum of the U.S. Army provided encouragement through the process and reviewed several early chapters. Jerry Holsworth of Winchester, Virginia, shared his library and was a constant source of encouragement. Gary Ecelbarger, my longtime friend in all things history, accompanied me on several field trips for this book, reviewed a critical chapter and offered tactical guidance in the course of writing this manuscript. The late Mr. Robert Messner of the Braddock Battlefield History Center assisted in accommodating several tour groups over the years, made the museum available on short notice on a few occasions and always shared his vast knowledge of Braddock's battlefield. Appreciation is also extended to George Chakvetadze, who completed the fine maps with short notice, and to the many others who contributed throughout the process. Last but not least, thanks are in order for editor Ryan Finn.

INTRODUCTION

Although technically at peace, Great Britain (England until 1707) and France had fought three wars with each other in North America in the sixty-five years leading up to the French and Indian War, which began in 1754. The belligerents fought King William's War from 1689 to 1697 in a conflict that ended with no material change to the North American territorial holdings of the two European powers. Peace lasted for fifteen years before conflict erupted again in 1702, igniting Queen Anne's War, the North American extension of the War of Spanish Succession. When that war ended, the Treaty of Utrecht gave Acadia (Nova Scotia), Newfoundland and Hudson Bay to the British and opened trade with American Indians to all nations, ending a French monopoly. The French also recognized English suzerainty over the Iroquois League. Peace reigned until 1744, when the European War of Austrian Succession spilled over to the colonies. The Treaty of Aix-la-Chapelle ended the war in 1748. However, simmering border issues in North America remained in flux, and the burgeoning population of British North America looked westward toward territories held by American Indians or the French, ensuring future conflict.

Both sides eyed the "Ohio Country," the land adjoining the Ohio River and its tributaries. As the Iroquois had long ago conquered the tribes in that coveted area, the English believed that the Trety of Utrecht gave them de facto control of the region. In Virginia, a group of influential colonists organized a venture for the purpose of settling that vast and promising territory. Their efforts succeeded on May 19, 1748, when King George II issued a Royal Charter signifying the incorporation of the Ohio Land Company. President of the Virginia Council Thomas Lee had conceived the idea in 1747 and organized interested investors to include Robert Dinwiddie, George Mason and Lawrence and Augustine Washington, George's elder brothers. The Royal Charter conditionally granted the company 500,000 acres along the Ohio River between the Kanawha and Monongahela Rivers. The charter required that the company settle one hundred families and "erect and maintain a fort" on the first 200,000 acres within seven years. If they succeeded in meeting those goals, the charter granted the company an additional 300,000 acres.[1]

Not all Virginians favored the Ohio Company, although its ownership included influential Virginia politicians whose personal interests often created a conflict of interest with their official duties. The company gave Lieutenant Governor Robert Dinwiddie a 5 percent stake in the entity, ensuring his cooperation. However, the House of Burgesses proved stubborn at times in supporting western expeditions funded by the colony, viewing it as a private venture attempting to advance its position on the backs of Virginia's landowners. There was also a competing interest in the settlement of the western regions claimed by Virginia, the Loyal Land Company, which included Thomas Jefferson's father, Peter, among its primary investors.

Additionally, the British cultivated economic relations via trade with the American Indians who inhabited the Ohio Country in the latter half of the 1740s. The British constructed trading posts at Pickawillany in modern Ohio, Logstown in Pennsylvania and Lower Shawnee Town on the Ohio River in what is now Kentucky. The Indians in these areas had traditionally been in the French sphere of influence, and their growing trade with Pennsylvania traders threatened the French hegemony. The resultant fur trade provided Pennsylvania with one-third of its exports. The superior quality of English trading goods over the French products quickly gained favor with the Ohio Country natives. "The English sparing nothing to keep them [the Indians] and to draw away the remainder of those who are here," complained a French officer in the region. He also observed that the excessive price of French products juxtaposed against the large gifts that the British made to the Indians "have entirely disposed those tribes in their favor." Moreover, he believed that the British were swaying the region's Indians "to bring them into a general revolt against the French." These developments alarmed French authorities in Quebec, who soon acted to protect their interests.[2]

ROBERT DINWIDDIE.
Governor of Virginia.

Lieutenant Governor Robert
Dinwiddie. *New York Public Library
Digital Collections.*

While the British and French vied for control of the region, the Iroquois League claimed the sparsely populated territory by right of conquest. Although they did not formally occupy the area in large numbers, the Iroquois exercised control over the region through its network of vassal tribes and allies, whose views were not always in sync with their overlords. The Iroquois League consisted of six tribes that controlled the Ohio lands from their stronghold in upstate New York. There they occupied lands from the Hudson River Valley to the shores of Lake Ontario to the west and governed from their council fires at Onondaga. Since the dawn of European settlement in North American, the Iroquois had walked a fine line between the English and French to maintain their power over other tribes, but by the time of the French and Indian War, most Iroquois were in the British camp. Conversely, tribes centered on the Great Lakes and within states that compose the modern American Midwest primarily allied with the French, in an area referred to as the "Pays d'en Haut."[3]

In 1748, the governor of New France, Roland-Michel Barrin de la Galissonière, reinforced the French claims to the region. While the British sought land for settlement, the French sought to maintain trade with the region's Indians and to secure their strategic lines of communication with French Louisiana via the Ohio and Mississippi Rivers. Galissonière ordered Captain Pierre-Joseph Celeron de Blainville, a French Marine officer, to lead an expedition of 250 French and Indians down the Ohio River to drive off British traders and formally mark the boundaries of French claims. Following an old European custom, Celeron buried six lead plates where major rivers flowed into the Ohio or Belle Riviere, an old European practice. Celeron traveled as far west as the Little Miami River, now the site of Cincinnati, Ohio, leaving the markers along the way. He also ordered British traders he encountered to leave the French claimed lands, but most simply ignored the edict and continued their activities unabated by the French. At least once, Indians angrily drove off the French party, rejecting their claims. The expedition returned to Montreal in November, having minimal impact on the competing claims to the Ohio Country.

Despite these French actions in the Ohio Country, the proprietors of the Ohio Company wasted little time in advancing their claims. In 1748, the company employed Colonel Thomas Cresap of Maryland, who with Delaware chief Nemacolin laid out "a rugged 60-mile trail" from the Potomac River to the Ohio Company's land grants along the Monongahela River. By 1749, they had constructed a storehouse across the Potomac River from the location of modern Cumberland, Maryland. There the Virginians stockpiled supplies and products to trade with the Indians. In 1750, the company hired Christopher Gist, an experienced frontiersman and native of Maryland, to explore the Ohio Country at the direction of Virginia's Lieutenant Governor Robert Dinwiddie. Gist's travels began in the fall of 1750 and carried him through land that now encompasses parts of Ohio, Kentucky, West Virginia, western Maryland and southwestern Pennsylvania.[4]

When the Ohio Company came calling in 1752 to discuss the British settlement with the Native Americans, chiefs accountable to Iroquois League in Onondaga called the shots. The lands along the upper Ohio River had long been the hunting ground of the Senecas, the westernmost of Iroquois tribes. Over time, some Seneca people had established a homeland between Lake Erie and the Allegheny River and became known as Mingos, their presence solidifying Iroquois claims to the region. Delawares and Shawnees, Iroquois vassal tribes pushed out of their lands in Pennsylvania by British settlement, settled the Ohio Valley in large numbers.[5]

The Ohio Company motivated politics in the Virginia Colony. "I have the success and prosperity of the Ohio Company much at heart," wrote Lieutenant Governor Dinwiddie to Thomas Cresap in early 1752. Dinwiddie hoped that Cresap, who had settled at Old Town on Maryland's western frontier, could enlist the assistance of the noted Indian leader of Pennsylvania Andrew Montour in negotiations.[6] In May 1752, Dinwiddie arranged a conference with the various tribes occupying the Ohio Country at Logstown on the Ohio River just south of the forks. Opening the territory southeast of the Ohio River, which had been granted to the Ohio Company for settlement, was the objective of the conference. Dinwiddie hired influential Indian interpreters George Croghan and Montour of Pennsylvania to facilitate the event. Joshua Fry, Lunsford Lomax and James Patton served as Virginia's official representatives, but Gist and Montour drove the English interests in the negotiations. Leaders of the Delaware, Shawnee and Mingo tribes attended, but Tanaghrisson, a Seneca or Mingo Half King from the Iroquois Confederacy, took on a leading role due to the Iroquois dominance over the regional tribes, who often disagreed with

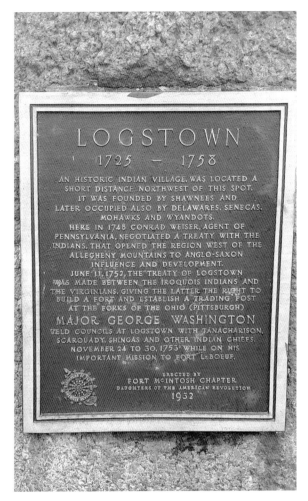

LOGSTOWN
1725 — 1758

AN HISTORIC INDIAN VILLAGE, WAS LOCATED A
SHORT DISTANCE NORTHWEST OF THIS SPOT.
IT WAS FOUNDED BY SHAWNEES AND
LATER OCCUPIED ALSO BY DELAWARES, SENECAS,
MOHAWKS AND WYANDOTS.
HERE IN 1748 CONRAD WEISER, AGENT OF
PENNSYLVANIA, NEGOTIATED A TREATY WITH THE
INDIANS, THAT OPENED THE REGION WEST OF THE
ALLEGHENY MOUNTAINS TO ANGLO-SAXON
INFLUENCE AND DEVELOPMENT.
JUNE 11, 1752, THE TREATY OF LOGSTOWN
WAS MADE BETWEEN THE IROQUOIS INDIANS AND
THE VIRGINIANS, GIVING THE LATTER THE RIGHT TO
BUILD A FORT AND ESTABLISH A TRADING POST
AT THE FORKS OF THE OHIO (PITTSBURGH)
MAJOR GEORGE WASHINGTON
HELD COUNCILS AT LOGSTOWN WITH TANACHARISON,
SCAROUADY, SHINGAS AND OTHER INDIAN CHIEFS,
NOVEMBER 24 TO 30, 1753, WHILE ON HIS
IMPORTANT MISSION TO FORT LeBOEUF.

ERECTED BY
FORT McINTOSH CHAPTER
DAUGHTERS OF THE AMERICAN REVOLUTION
1932

This page: This marker denotes the location of the Native American village of Logstown on the Ohio River where the 1752 Logstown conference occurred and where Washington met Tanaghrisson in 1753 at the outset of his journey to the French forts. *Photos by Harry Smeltzer.*

him. After private discussion with Mountour, Tanaghrisson and the other Iroquois leaders eventually agreed to British settlement of the area southeast of the Ohio River, although the tribes who lived there, the Delawares and Shawnees, were not consulted. Such settlement would improve trade between the English and the Indians and would allow the English to more closely support their perceived Native American neighbors against threats from the French and their Indian allies. Not only did Tanaghrisson agree to allow the English settlement, but he also privately affirmed the controversial Treaty of Lancaster, which the Delawares had never accepted, as it had been foisted on them by their Iroquois overlords. Half King Tanaghrisson had played a delicate balancing act at Logstown. Historian Colin Galloway observed that he "managed to present himself as a friend to the English, loyal representative of Onondaga, and a defender of the Ohio Indian rights and lands."[7]

Even before the results of the Logstown Conference were known, the French undertook more serious measures to rid the region of the British influence. Charles Michel de Langlade, the son of a French Canadian fur trader and an Ottawa Indian woman, raided Pickawillany, a Miami Indian village and a British trading post in modern Ohio, eight days after the Logstown Conference concluded. Langlade led 30 French soldiers from Fort Detroit and 201 Ottawa and Ojibwa warriors in an attack against the village on June 21, 1752. The French party easily gained the upper hand, as most of the village's warriors were absent on a hunting trip. After the surrender, the French-allied Indians killed a wounded British trader and ate his heart. They then boiled alive and ate the elderly chief of Pickawillany. Langlade's party burned and destroyed "one of the largest settlements and the richest trading post west of the Appalachians." The French took five British traders prisoner and marched them back to Fort Detroit. Langlade's Raid soon had the desired effect on both the Indians and the British. The Pennsylvania traders who had flooded into the region quickly packed up and returned to their homes. The Miamis pleaded with Pennsylvania and Virginia for aid, but the distant English moved slowly through their bureaucratic channels and the Miami tribe did not receive the support needed to remain in the British orbit.[8]

Nearly three months after the attack, Dinwiddie informed the board of trade in London of the Logstown treaty and the situation of the Miami nation, although he did not know about Pickawillany. They "have taken up the hatchet (as they term it) against the French and the Indians in amity with them." By December 10, Dinwiddie had learned of the full details of

Pickawillany when Captain William Trent returned from his expedition west of the Ohio to deliver gifts to the Miami people. He found them in "miserable condition…their town taken, and many of their people killed by the French and Indians in amity with them, and many of the English traders ruined, being robbed of their goods, some killed, and others carried away [as] prisoners." "They have applied to me for protection, and power to make reprisals, which I by no means would grant, as we are at peace with the French, but I pray your Lordships' directions on how to behave on such applications for the future, as I think the British subjects are under great oppression and severities from the French traders in their villainous robberies."

Dinwiddie determined to send the Miamis and the Iroquois "twenty barrels of gunpowder, one hundred small arms, and some clothing" in the spring. He also related stories of the French from Fort Detroit promising Indians "one hundred crowns for every white scalp they bring them." Dinwiddie believed that "it will be of great service to confirm them to our interest, as they will be a great protection to our back settlements to the westward. They could also disrupt communications between French Canada and Louisiana." Dinwiddie decided that the time had arrived to construct forts in the Ohio Country to defend British interests. The letter eventually made its way to King George II, as the issue Dinwiddie outlined "appears to be a matter of a very tender nature."[9]

In 1753, the French moved significant military assets into the Ohio Country. In addition to countering the threat posed by the English, they wanted to ensure that the strong Miami tribe did not sever Fort Detroit from eastern New France. Under orders from the governor of New France, Michel-Ange Duquesne, Marquis de Menneville, French troops constructed Fort Presque Isle at what is now Erie, Pennsylvania; Fort Le Boeuf, fifteen miles southward at modern Waterford; and eventually Fort Machault, on the west side of the Allegheny River near present-day Franklin, Pennsylvania. A French officer led a detachment of marines and allied Seneca Indians in a show of force to the various tribes along the Allegheny and Ohio Rivers. Realizing the French military might, the Miami tribe quickly returned to the French orbit.[10]

In September 1753, Dinwiddie organized a conference with many of the Ohio Country Indians at Winchester in the northern Shenandoah Valley at the western edge of British settlement to solidify the 1752 Logstown Treaty and secure their alliance against the French. The Virginians promised the Native Americans "a suitable quantity of ammunition" that would be stored for them in a secure place east of the Ohio. Trusted agents Christopher Gist, William Trent and Andrew Mountour managed these stores and distributed them to the tribes "as their occasions and Behaviour should require." The Virginians also promised to appropriate "a large sum of Money for the use of these Indians, in case they should be distressed by their Enemies, and their Hunting and Planting prevented."[11]

Dinwiddie kept his superiors in London informed of these developments. The Virginia governor received a reply to his missive in October 1753. King George II himself directed Dinwiddie and the other colonial governors to require any "Indians or Europeans" building forts in Virginia (which included the disputed Ohio Country) to "peaceably depart." If they failed to obey and continued "any such unlawful and unjustifiable Designs," the king commanded Dinwiddie "to drive them off by Force of Arms."[12]

At Williamsburg on November 1, 1753, Dinwiddie addressed the Virginia House of Burgesses at the king's direction. He advised them that "a large Body of French regulars and Ind's…marched from Canada to the river Ohio in a hostile manner, to invade His Majesty's Territories." If that were not enough, these French had the gall to construct a fort "on His Majesty's Land." Dinwiddie told the burgesses that the king had exhorted them "to grant such Supplies as the Exigency of the present Affairs requires." He also revealed that the king was sending thirty cannons with ammunition to protect the frontier. When the legislative session closed on December 18 with no resolution, Dinwiddie scolded them, warning that their disregard of the French actions "may be of bad consequence." Regardless of the burgesses' inaction, Dinwiddie doggedly pursued his efforts to confront the French in the Ohio Country.[13]

Chapter 1

"ESPECIAL TRUST & CONFIDENCE"

Messenger for the Governor

Although the Virginia Assembly failed to back Dinwiddie during its late 1753 session, the shrewd Scotsman had already enacted his plan. On October 30, 1753, he appointed twenty-one-year-old Major George Washington to deliver a summons to the French commandant at Fort Le Boeuf (now Waterford, Pennsylvania) just south of Erie. In addition to the summons, Dinwiddie desired Washington to introduce himself to several prominent Indian chiefs at Logstown on the Ohio River and apprise them of his mission. The objective was to obtain a detachment of warriors to escort Washington and serve as his "Safeguard." Dinwiddie also instructed Washington to "diligently enquire into the Numbers & Force of the French on the Ohio…take Care to be truly informed what Forts the French have erected, & where; How they are Garrisoned & appointed.…And from the best Intelligence You can procure, you are to learn what gave Occasion to this expedition of the French. How they are likely to be supported, & what their Pretentions are." In short, Washington functioned as both a diplomat and a spy on this mission.[14]

At this point, the youthful Major George Washington who departed Williamsburg was not the man we know who led the Continental army to victory in the American Revolution and became our first president. Instead, we find an ambitious yet insecure and inexperienced young man seeking to find his place in the world. Author Peter Stark observed, "Everything about Washington's life played out on a grander scale than most people's, including his maturing during his younger years." Stark further noted that while most people make mistakes as they mature and grow from them, Washington's missteps "occurred in an arena that quickly expanded from local, to regional and finally to global with far reaching historical consequences."[15]

George Washington was born in 1732 a member of the fourth generation of Washingtons in the Virginia Colony. Washington was the first child of his father, Augustine, and his third wife, Mary Ball. His father died eleven years later, and George grew close to his older half brother Lawrence, who provided the boy with a mentor and role model George greatly admired. Given the influence and connections that Lawrence provided his brother, a brief discussion of his life is in order.

Lawrence was the heir to Augustine Washington's estates, being fourteen years George's senior. Both Lawrence and his brother Augustine Jr. received extensive educations in England, an advantage the younger George did not receive. After nine years in England, Lawrence returned to manage his father's two-thousand-acre plantation on Little Hunting Creek that would later become Mount Vernon. Lawrence also met his six-year-old half brother for the first time and quickly became the object of George's admiration. In 1742, Lawrence served as an officer in a newly created 43rd Regiment of Foot during the War for Jenkins' Ear. He received an appointment as captain of the foot soldiers selected to act as marines on Admiral Edward Vernon's flagship during the failed British attacks on Cartagena, New Granada, Cuba and Panama. During this war, the British suffered heavy losses from disease. Washington's assignment aboard the admiral's flagship saved him from yellow fever that killed off nearly 90 percent of the Virginians on the troop ships. While Lawrence avoided the tropical fevers, he contracted tuberculosis, which would ultimately take his life.[16]

When he returned to Virginia, he became militia commander of the Northern Neck. He resided on the family's Little Hunting Creek estate. In 1743, he married Anne "Nancy" Fairfax, daughter of the wealthy and influential Colonel William Fairfax, who resided at the neighboring Belvoir plantation. Lawrence's marriage into a family of the British aristocracy was a major step up for him, and this union opened many doors for himself and, later, George. Through this marriage, George became closely acquainted with the Fairfax family, including Colonel Fairfax and his son George William, as well as Lord Fairfax himself. Marrying into wealth and land had long been a trait of Washington men, and George would later follow that path. Lawrence also became involved in politics, serving in the Virginia House of Burgesses as a representative for Fairfax County.

Ruins of Joist Hite's house and tavern, circa 1730s, south of Winchester, Virginia. Washington lodged here as a young surveyor in 1748. *Author photo.*

Springdale, home of the Hite family, located on Opequon Creek in southern Frederick County, Virginia, was constructed in 1753 and visited by Colonel Washington during the French and Indian War. *Author photo.*

Lawrence was also a key investor in the Ohio Company along with his brother Augustine. Those lands belonged to Lord Fairfax. When Lord Fairfax's agent, his nephew George William Fairfax, set out to survey the Lord's western lands, he included George Washington on the crew. He had inherited his father's surveying tools, and Lawrence tutored both Georges in trigonometry. In March 1748, the younger Washington traveled with George Fairfax across the Blue Ridge Mountains and into the Shenandoah Valley, arriving at Lord Fairfax's keep at Greenway Court, sending their baggage ahead to Captain Joist Hite's homestead near Fredericktown, now Winchester, Virginia.

Surveying exposed Washington to the rugged life of living and working on the frontier. Staying at a crude homestead, Washington noted his inexperience in matters when he stripped himself down "very orderly" in preparation for sleep. When he "went in the bed as they called it," he was surprised to see it consisting of "nothing but a little straw—matted together without sheets or anything else but one thread bear blanket with double its weight of vermin such as lice, fleas & c." He quickly put on his clothes but noted, "Had we have not been very tired, I am sure we should not have slept so much." He also promised himself to "sleep in the open air before a fire" and never again utilize such unseemly quarters. The following morning, Washington and his comrades "cleaned ourselves to get rid of the game we had catched the night before."[17]

Washington's work also took him to Colonel Thomas Cresap's settlement at Oldtown in Maryland. To get there, Washington swam his horse across the rain-swollen Potomac River and then proceeded forty miles westward on what he believed was "the worst road that was ever trod by man or beast." At Cresap's, Washington encountered his first Indians. "We were agreeably surprised at the sight of thirty odd Indians coming from war with only one scalp," he noted in his diary. They shared their liquor with the Indians, "elevating their spirits," which "put them in the humor of dancing."[18] He watched them form a large circle with a "great fire in the middle." When it started, George thought "the best dancer jumps up as one awaked out of a sleep and runs and jumps about the ring in a most comical manner" followed by the others, moving rhythmically to the beat of a primitive drum and a crude rattle.[19]

Washington's surveying work exposed him to life on the frontier, and he took well to it. Hunting for wild turkey, sleeping in a tent and living in the sometimes-harsh weather conditions readied him for his future in the military, although he did not know it at the time. He met many families in

Monument to Washington the surveyor, located at Washington's Office in Winchester, Virginia. *Author photo.*

View toward Potomac River from Cresap's Fort. Perhaps Washington witnessed the Indian dancing in this area. *Author photo.*

the Shenandoah Valley and the mountains beyond in what is now western Maryland and West Virginia. Ultimately, Washington conducted 190 surveys from 1748 to 1751, most of them for land grants located on the frontier of Lord Fairfax's Northern Neck Proprietary. With this experience, Washington also became the official county surveyor for Culpeper County, even though he did not reside there. Washington also used this time to purchase thousands of acres of land in the Shenandoah Valley and on the frontier.

During this time, Lawrence's health continually deteriorated, a complication of the affliction he contracted during the War of Jenkins' Ear. In search of relief, Lawrence traveled to Barbados in the West Indies, taking brother George along on the journey. In Barbados, a doctor assured Lawrence that his condition was curable. The Washingtons resided in a home that overlooked Carlisle Bay in Bridgetown, the largest city George had ever seen. He found himself in the company of the upper crust of British society. Although the warm climate of the Caribbean was intended to heal Lawrence, his health continued to decline, and George caught a mild case of smallpox. The stay in Barbados was not improving Lawrence's health. Although Barbados was "the finest island of the West Indies," Lawrence complained, that "no place can please me without a change of seasons." The intense heat particularly bothered him, and the expected health benefits did not materialize. Lawrence had sent George home to Virginia by December 19, 1751, and moved himself to Bermuda in the hopes that the climate there would be more suitable for his condition.[20]

The six weeks in Bridgetown left an indelible impression on the younger Washington. They rented a home from a British army officer and traveled into town nearly every day for a dinner invitation. Living in a major economic center of the British empire challenged his worldviews and elevated his life's ambition. He regularly dined with the upper crust members of society and was astounded at being treated as an equal. He wrote that "hospitality and genteel behavior" was shown to "every gentleman stranger by the gentleman inhabitants." During his stay, George dined with a colonial governor, naval commodore and an army general. He also explored the island, noting that it was "one entire fortification." His mind drifted to the military activity on the island, and he noted the number of guns and types of fortifications that he observed. This experience fostered or enhanced his desire to obtain a commission in the British army. Overall, it was probably the most wondrous time George had experienced thus far in his young life, but after six weeks it came to an end and he sailed back to Virginia.[21]

George disembarked at Yorktown, where he later forced the surrender of Lord Cornwallis's army in 1781 to achieve victory in the American Revolution. Washington hastened to Williamsburg, which previously had been the largest town or city that had seen before visiting Bridgetown. Now he sarcastically referred to the provincial capital of Virginia as "the great metropolis." He stopped at the Governor's Palace to deliver letters to Lieutenant Governor Robert Dinwiddie. Eager for news from Barbados and an associate of Lawrence's, the governor invited George to dinner, providing the young Virginian an opportunity to practice the social etiquette that he experienced at Bridgetown. This meeting of Dinwiddie and Washington produced no notable outcomes, but it did portend the development of relationship that later helped to ignite the French and Indian War. Before long, Dinwiddie called on Washington to carry out crucial missions on behalf of the colony and the Crown.[22]

From Williamsburg, he traveled north to Mount Vernon, where Lawrence later joined him. The Caribbean climate had provided no respite from the tuberculosis that was sapping his life away. He spent his remaining time with his wife, Nancy; infant daughter; George; and other members of the Washington family. Lawrence died on July 26, 1752, a harsh blow to George, who had idolized his older brother. George Mason consoled George on his loss: "I most heartily console you on the loss of so worthy a brother and friend." Washington eventually inherited Mount Vernon, but it came at the cost of the lives of his brother and his wife.

In 1752, George Washington was seeking to gain military experience and actively sought the adjutancy of the Northern Neck militia. The position carried the rank of major and the responsibility of training the militia. Lawrence had served as Virginia's adjutant general, but poor health limited his service. Dinwiddie commissioned George the adjutant of the militia for the Southern District of Virginia on December 13, 1752. It was an important step and a sign of his growing favor with the lieutenant governor. Soon George was summoned for an assignment that forever changed his life. The French incursion and construction of several forts between Lake Erie and the Forks of the Ohio and the king's direction to order the French off British territory pushed Dinwiddie to action. On October 30, 1753, he charged Major Washington with the biggest assignment of his young life. Dinwiddie placed "especial trust" and confidence in "the ability, conduct and fidelity of you, the said George Washington" and appointed him express messenger for the governor.[23] He directed George to travel to Logstown on the Ohio River and learn the location of the French forces. There he should inform the Half King, Tanaghrisson, Monacatoocha and the other chiefs of his mission and ask them for warriors to serve as an escort. Dinwiddie directed him to then proceed to the French fort and present his credentials and "my letter to the chief commanding officer, and in the name of his Britannic Majesty, to demand an answer from him thereto." Furthermore, George was to spy on the French, learning all that he could about the dispositions of the French forces, their forts, their plans and their communications with Canada.

Washington departed Williamsburg on October 31, stopping the next day in Fredericksburg, where he hired Jacob Van Braam, an immigrant from Holland, to serve as interpreter with the French. They rode to Alexandria, purchased supplies and then continued to Winchester, where they obtained packhorses to carry baggage and supplies. They made their way to the Ohio Company storehouse at Wills Creek, now Cumberland, Maryland, arriving on November 14. He hired Christopher Gist as his guide and four other experienced traders to lead him through the Ohio Country. The journey was not easy, as "excessive rains and vast quantities of snow" turned the small tracks that served as roads into muddy, slippery quagmires and made the men miserable.[24]

Traveling by canoe up the Monongahela River, Washington passed the Forks of the Ohio, and his surveying instincts emerged. He observed "the Land in the Fork, which I think extremely well situated for a Fort, as it has the absolute Command of both Rivers." He also studied the ground where the Ohio Company planned to build its fort downstream from the forks. "My Judgement [is] to think it greatly inferior, either for Defense or Advantages." He also came across four French deserters who had come up the Mississippi and Ohio Rivers from New Orleans. He promptly queried them for particulars on the French forts and military strength throughout the regions they had traveled through and promptly wrote down every detail in his journal, revealing an eye for military details.[25] Washington soon learned that the French commander, Pierre Paul de La Malgue, had died at Fort Le Boeuf on October 29 and that the French had sent the larger portion of their forces into winter quarters at Montreal, leaving only a small garrison at the forts in the Ohio Country.

Washington wasted no time in following Dinwiddie's directions to meet with the Indians at Logstown. In the process, he gained experience in dealing with the local Native Americans, calling several important leaders to a council at Logstown on the Ohio River on November 26. There he met Tanaghrisson, the Seneca Half King representing the Iroquois Nation from Onondaga, New York, the Iroquois center of power and a man who would soon become Washington's closet Native American ally. Also present was Monacatoocha, an Oneida chief whom the Iroquois appointed to oversee their vassal tribal, the Shawnees, and Shingas, king of the Delawares. This was Washington's first experience dealing with the Native Americans, but he confidently addressed them on the details of his mission and need for their assistance.[26]

After some discussion among the Indians, the Half King arose and assured Washington, "You may depend that we will endeavor to be your Guard." Unfortunately, the Half King would require three days of preparations. Washington replied that his orders did not permit him time to delay, annoying the Half King. Realizing that Indians would be greatly offended by a sudden departure, Washington "consented to stay." In the end, the Indians failed to deliver the desired manpower to safeguard Washington's party to the French forts. Only the Half King and "two old men and one young warrior" accompanied Washington's party. This would not be the last time that Tanaghrisson failed to deliver promised manpower.[27]

After a cold, wet journey over difficult terrain, Washington arrived at Fort Machault on December 5. The French officers occupied the house

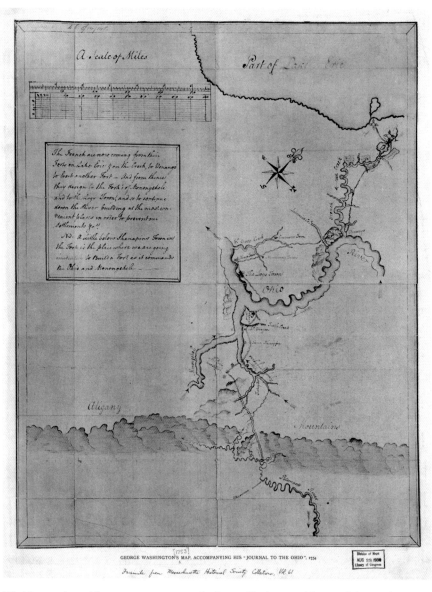

Washington drew this map to accompany the journal he kept on his expedition to the French forts in late 1753. *Library of Congress.*

of English trader John Frazier, whom they had driven off earlier in the year. With French colors flying over the home, the commander, Captain Phillippe Thomas de Joncaire, Sieur de Chabert, of the French Marines, greeted Washington and Gist "kindly and complacently." They refused to accept Dinwiddie's message, declaring that Washington must travel fifteen miles northward to Fort Le Boeuf and deliver the ultimatum to the French commander. Among the officers at Machault was Michel Pepin, known as Monsieur La Force on the frontier, noted for his interpretive skills and diplomacy with the Native Americans. The French invited Washington to dinner and "dosed themselves pretty plentifully" with wine. The French imbibing soon "gave license to their tongues to review their sentiments more freely." They declared that they would "take possession of the Ohio, & by G-- they would do it." They acknowledged that the English outnumbered the French but believed "their [English] Motions were too slow & dilatory to prevent any Undertaking of theirs [French]." They expressed, or "pretended" as Washington considered it, the "undoubted right to the river" by LaSalle's expedition. Washington also learned that a large part of the French troops had temporarily withdrawn northward to their main forts for winter.[28]

On November 7, Washington's party departed Venango (Fort Machault) for Fort Le Boeuf escorted by Monsieur La Force and three French soldiers. "Excessive rains, Snows, & bad traveling through many Mires & Swamps" slowed their progress and made the journey a difficult and unpleasant voyage. Upon arriving at the fort, the commander notified Washington that only Captain Jacques LeGardeur, Sieur de Saint Pierre, the commandant of French forces in the Ohio Country, could accept Dinwiddie's demand letter. However, he had not yet arrived, and Washington waited. When St. Pierre showed up the next day at 2:00 p.m., he impressed Washington as "an elderly gentleman and has much the air of a soldier." Washington had aptly read St. Pierre, a veteran of thirty years in the French Marine companies of North America who had much combat experience against both Indians and the British during King George's War. He would be killed in battle at Lac du St. Sacrement (Lake George) in 1755. St. Pierre readily accepted the letter and then excused himself. An interpreter translated Dinwiddie's demands for St. Pierre and his officers. Meanwhile, Washington studied the fort, its armaments and manpower and instructed his men to get an exact count of the canoes on hand that would convey the French to the forks the following spring.[29] He observed that the fort was "situated on the South or West fork of French Creek, near the water and is

29

almost surrounded by the Creek and a small branch of it which forms kind of an island" and took detailed notes on its design and weapons.[30]

That evening, St. Pierre handed Washington a written reply to the demand letter. He complained that Washington should have been ordered to the French general, "to whom it belongs rather than me, to set forth the evidence and the reality of the rights of the King, my master, to the lands situation along the Belle Riviere, and to contest the pretensions of the King of Great Britain, thereto." Washington had evidently impressed St. Pierre, for he wrote to Dinwiddie, "I have made it a particular duty to receive Mr. Washington with the distinction owing to your dignity, his position and his own great merit"—powerful words from a man of St. Pierre's experience.[31]

Washington departed on Fort Le Boeuf on December 16. He had hoped to leave sooner, but his Native American companions desired to stay the previous night to receive guns and other gifts from the French. After the Indians received the promised goods, the French attempted to ply them with liquor, but Washington steadfastly held the Half King to his promise to depart that morning. They had "a tedious and very fatiguing passage down the creek." Rocks and shallow shoals prompted them to exit their canoes and carry them over the shallows, forcing them to wade in the cold water "an half hour or more." They did not arrive at Venango until December 22. One of the Half King's men injured himself and was unable to continue the journey, so Washington and Gist continued without their Native American contingent. The pace proved much too slow for Washington, who desired to get the French reply to Dinwiddie in Williamsburg. On December 24, he and Gist left the interpreter Van Braam and the rest of the party behind at Venango. Washington and Gist also abandoned their horses, as the animals were too weak to continue the journey.

Washington insisted that Gist accompany him on foot, "as the creeks were frozen and our horses could make but little way." Gist initially declined because Washington "had never been used to walking before this time." However, Washington insisted, and they set out "dressed like Indians with our packs," journeying through the cold winter. On December 27, they encountered a Native American, who greeted Gist by his Indian name and who agreed to lead them by the shortest route to the Forks of the Ohio. The inexperienced Virginian tired, and the Indian voluntarily carried Washington's pack. They covered nine miles at a rapid pace, and Washington's feet "grew very sore, and he very weary." Even worse, the Indian had steered too far to the northeast. The fatigued Washington wanted to camp for the night, and the Indian volunteered to tend to the Virginian's musket, which was prudently refused. Gist wrote, "Then the Indian became churlish and pressed us to keep on, telling us that there were Ottawa Indians in these woods, and they would scalp us if we lay out." Instead, he insisted that they go to his cabin, which he explained was within hearing distance of a musket shot.[32]

Veteran frontiersman Gist did not trust the Indian and "thought very ill of the fellow but did not care to let the Major know I mistrusted him." After going on for several miles, Washington ordered that they stop for the night at the next waterway. As they entered an open meadow dusted with a light snow, the Indian whirled around and fired his gun toward Washington and Gist. Washington called out, "Are you shot?" "No," replied Gist. The Indian attempted to hide behind a tree and reload, but Washington and Gist quickly subdued him. Gist wanted to shoot him, but Major Washington did not permit it, perhaps hoping to avoid an incident with the Natives at a time when the Virginians were trying to cultivate alliances. Eventually, they let him go but continued walking through the night, fearing that he would return with more warriors. On December 29, they crafted a log raft to cross the Allegheny River and got over to an island "with much difficulty." "We expected every moment our raft would sink, and we would perish," wrote Washington in his journal. The swift waters of the Allegheny and chunks of floating ice made navigation almost impossible. Washington planted his pole in the riverbed to stop the raft, but the "rapidity of the stream threw it [the raft] with so much violence against the pole, that it jerked me into ten feet [of] water." The young major latched on to one of the logs and saved himself. The raft was lost, and they waded to shore on the island. Gist's fingers were frostbitten, and Washington was frigidly soaked to the bone, so they spent the night on the island, warming themselves by a fire. By morning, the river had frozen over, and they walked across the ice.[33]

They passed the forks and traveled ten miles to Turtle Creek on the Monongahela River, spending the night at John Frazier's newly constructed trading post. There they enjoyed a much welcome rest. While they waited to obtain horses at Frazier's, Washington and Gist traveled three miles upstream until they reached the mouth of the Youghiogheny River, where they visited Queen Alliquippa of the Mingo Indians. She "expressed great concern that we passed her in going to the [French] Fort," but Washington smoothed over the situation by presenting her with a long match coat and a bottle of rum, "which was thought much the better present of the two." The queen opined that "she would never go down the river Allegheny to live, except [if] the English built a fort, then she would go and live there."[34]

Washington and Gist visit Queen Alliquippa during their trip from the French forts in 1753. *Miriam and Ira D. Wallach Division of Art, Prints and Photographs: Print Collection, New York Public Library Digital Collections.*

On January 1, 1754, they rode fresh horses from Frazier's and reached Gist's settlement, located just north of what is now Uniontown, Pennsylvania. A few days later, they passed a party with seventeen packhorses loaded with materials to build a storehouse at Redstone Creek on the Monongahela, the beginning of the English response to the French advances. They finally arrived at the Ohio Company storehouse at Wills Creek on January 6. "There was but one day," complained Washington, "but it rained or snowed incessantly and throughout the whole journey we met with nothing but one continued series of cold wet weather, which occasioned very uncomfortable lodgings." Washington made it to Belvoir, the Fairfax family home, on January 11, where he stopped "one day to take necessary rest." Then he continued on to Williamsburg, where he arrived on January 16 and presented the French response to Dinwiddie.[35]

Chapter 2

"I HAVE THE AFFAIRS OF THE OHIO MUCH AT HEART"

Lieutenant Governor Dinwiddie Prepares for War

Upon arriving in Williamsburg, Major Washington promptly visited Governor Dinwiddie at the Governor's Palace. He brought the French commander's refusal of Dinwiddie's demands and Washington's detailed account of the entire expedition. Five days later, Dinwiddie apprised the Virginia Council of the French refusal and developments resulting from Washington's mission. In response to the French military presence, this council recommended the recruitment of one hundred men from the Shenandoah Valley counties of Frederick and Augusta. Most notably, Major Washington was to assume command of the company, march to the Ohio Country and confront the French.

On January 29, Dinwiddie composed a dispatch to London telling Secretary of State Holderness and the board of trade that the French had indeed penetrated the Ohio Country. He further wrote that they had begun construction on Fort Machault and planned to build more. He detailed the strength of their forces, "understood would be fifteen hundred regulars, besides Indians," equipped with three hundred canoes and bateaux to carry the men and supplies down river to the forks in March.[36] Dinwiddie commissioned Captain William Trent to recruit a company of one hundred men among the traders and woodsmen of Augusta County and "the exterior Settlements of this Dominion." A native of Lancaster, Pennsylvania, Trent had military experience in 1746 during King George's War with the French and had also made his mark as a capable frontiersman. Critically for the mission at hand, he knew the settlers of the backcountry and had cultivated established relationships with the Indians of the Ohio Country attained during his extensive trading activities. He had also served as a formal liaison between the Pennsylvania Assembly and the tribes in the region, further solidifying his credentials with the Native Americans. Trent received bold and clear instructions from Dinwiddie, who harbored no qualms ordering the use of force against the French. The lieutenant governor wrote, "As You have a good Interest with the Indians, I doubt not You will prevail with many of them to join You in order to defeat the Designs of the French in taking their Lands from them by force of Arms." He further directed Trent to "dislodge and drive away [the French], and in case of refusal and resistance to kill and destroy or take Prisoners all and every Person and Persons not Subjects of the King of G.B. who now are or shall hereafter come to settle and take Possession of any Lands on said River Ohio."[37]

Lieutenant Governor Dinwiddie raised the stakes in the Ohio Country. He determined to confront the French military advance into the region with a force of Virginians. In late January, he informed the influential William Fairfax of his intentions in a letter carried north to Belvoir by Fairfax's neighbor Washington. "[I] have Commissioned Major Washington to enlist 100 Men from the Militia of Augusta and Frederick and Capt. Wm. Trent has my Commission to enlist 100 more among the Traders &c.; these two Companies to march directly after raised, to protect and assist them in building the Fort. And as I have called the Assembly to meet the 14th of next Mo. I hope they will enable me to raise 400 Men more to go out early in the Spring, and I shall write to the neighboring Governments to assist us… these Forces with the Conjunction of our friendly Indians I hope will make a good Appearance on the Ohio and be able to defeat the Designs of the French." Dinwiddie emphasized to Fairfax, "I have the affairs of the Ohio much at Heart, [and] if the Burgesses come in good Temper to do what is their Duty to the Crown and in Protection of their Country, I hope we shall be able to convince the French we are not always slow in our Motions." Given that Dinwiddie clearly knew that there were already three hundred French regulars in theater, with more soon to arrive, sending two hundred inexperienced recruits under Washington and Trent to check French designs was an exceptionally inadequate measure.[38]

Dinwiddie believed that he would find many willing allies among the Native Americans in the Ohio Country to oppose the French. He wrote to the chiefs, "I have therefore thought proper as your good Friend and Brother to let You know that I have given Command and Orders to my officers to join You with some Forces if you will take the Hatchet into your hands." He added, "And as there is no question but that Your enemy [the French] may be now easily driven away if not suffered to become more numerous, but immediately to send out Your Warriors; to whose assistance I propose in a short Time to send a considerable Number of our soldiers." In short, Dinwiddie encouraged the Iroquois to attack the French and promised the assistance of Washington's and Trent's commands.[39]

Dinwiddie ordered Washington, eager to gain a military reputation, to rush to Winchester in the northern Shenandoah Valley and take charge of one hundred men from Frederick and Augusta Counties. "Train and discipline them in the best Manner You can," directed Dinwiddie. He assigned John Carlisle at Alexandria to provide Washington with the supplies that he needed to build his command and conduct his mission. Dinwiddie ordered Washington to quickly march to the Forks of Ohio and to expedite the construction of the fort that Captain Trent will have begun by the time George arrived. Most importantly, Dinwiddie clearly delineated Washington's rules of engagement (author's emphasis): "*You are to act on the Defensive, but in Case any Attempts are made to obstruct the Works or interrupt our Settlements by any Persons whatsoever You are to restrain all such Offenders, and in Case of resistance to make Prisoners of or kill and destroy them.* For the rest, you are to conduct yourself as the Circumstances of the Service shall require and to act as You shall find best for the Furtherance of His Majesty's Service and the Good of His Dominion. Wishing Your Health and Success, I bid You Farewell."[40]

At the recommendation of Colonel Fairfax, Dinwiddie appointed John Carlyle, a prosperous Scottish merchant who resided in Alexandria, Virginia, as a major and "Commissary of Stores and Provisions for the Supply of Forces designed for the river Ohio." Dinwiddie directed Carlyle to "procure a sufficient Quantity of Flower, Bread, Beef and Pork for 500 men for six or eight Months." Dinwiddie noted that he would send Carlyle ten cannons and two hundred muskets to equip Washington's command. For transporting the supplies, he empowered Carlyle to impress "Boats, Wagons, Carts, Horses &c…unless You can hire at reasonable rates." The governor's instructions proved highly optimistic and unrealistic in both terms of the number of men who could be recruited for the effort as well as Carlyle's ability to supply an expedition deep into the wilderness of North America.[41]

Dinwiddie informed his fellow royal governors in the colonies, rallying them against the French and seeking their support for his military initiative to the Forks of the Ohio. He explained Washington's expedition to the French commander, as well as the realization that the French were preparing for an advance down the Ohio in the spring of 1754 and rallying their Indian allies to their cause. Dinwiddie requested troops and money from the colonial governors, but in the end, only one Independent Company of British Regulars arrived from South Carolina in time to take part in the campaign.

Washington's Attempts to Raise a Regiment

By February 19, Captain Trent had joined Christopher Gist at the Forks of the Ohio. He informed Washington that he expected "all the people," including the Half King, to arrive there in a few days. Then they would lay the foundation for the British fort. Trent urged that Washington "march out to them with all possible expedition." Captain La Force had warned the British aligned Native Americans "that either they nor the English there, would see the sun above twenty days longer; thirteen of the days being then to come." Pennsylvania Indian agent and frontier trader George Croghan warned Trent that "they might expect 400 French down [the Ohio River] in that time." Washington would need to act quickly if Dinwiddie's plans for a British fort at the forks to succeed.[42]

In compliance with Dinwiddie's orders, Washington traveled in wintry conditions to Winchester, where he attempted to raise one hundred men from the militias of Augusta and Frederick Counties in the Shenandoah Valley. Washington's attempt came on the heels of Trent already trying to raise one hundred men from Augusta County and the frontier to the west. To entice men into active service in the untamed Ohio Country, Dinwiddie set aside vast acreages "of His Majesty the king of Great Britain's…and granted to such persons, who by the voluntary engagement and good behavior in the said service shall deserve the same." Despite the potential reward, Washington failed to meet his recruitment goals in the Shenandoah Valley due to a lack of support by the local militia officers. By early March, he had returned to Northern Virginia. On March 9, from Alexandria, he told Dinwiddie, "I have increased my number of men to about 25." He added that there would have been more if not for the "excessive" bad weather. Disappointed at the lack of recruits from the Shenandoah, Dinwiddie wrote to Lord Fairfax, lieutenant of the militia in the Shenandoah Valley, "I…am sorry the first Orders I gave in respect to the Militia should meet with such disrespect in a County under your Lordship's command.…Let the Delinquents know I am much offended at the disrespect shewn to my Orders, especially at this critical time." Dinwiddie directed that the offending officers be cashiered from the militia and sent Fairfax six blank commissions "to be filled up as You see proper, and [I] hope to such Persons as will be obedient to Commands."[43]

Washington noted that those men who did enlist "are much in want of and press greatly for clothing." Washington informed Dinwiddie, "They all desire so earnestly to be put into a uniform dress that they would gladly do it at their own expense to be deducted out of their pay [that] it was their greatest objection to enlisting and many have refused solely on that account after coming purposely to do it with expectation of getting a regimental suit." He further described the recruits as "idle persons that are quite destitute of house, and home, and I may truly say many of them of clothes, which last, renders them very incapable of the necessary service, as they must unavoidably be exposed to inclement weather in their Marches.…There is many of them without shoes, other's want stockings." Washington further asserted that providing the men with formal British uniforms would give the Indians "a much higher conception of our power and greatness." Even if Dinwiddie could only provide a "coat of the coarsest red," it would satisfy the men's wishes and impress the Natives, who compared red to blood and would look on the crimson uniforms "as the distinguishing marks of warriors and great men." For good measure, Washington added that "the shabby and ragged appearance of the French common soldiers make affords great matter for ridicule among the Indians, and I really believe is the chief motive why they hate and despise them as they do." Washington's notions regarding the sentiments of Native Americans exposed his inexperience and his ignorance of the deep ties that already existed between the French and many tribes.[44]

Meanwhile, Dinwiddie had been pondering the situation and sent Lord Holdernesse a letter on the developing situation. He lamented the failure of the Virginia militia to turn out for the campaign but concluded, "I think 300 men raised voluntarily will do more service than 800 men of the militia forced on the service." The Virginia governor recognized that the French military tradition in Canada gave them an inherent advantage in experience. "If I had one regiment of regular troops," wrote Dinwiddie, "I should not doubt of answering our intention of building forts and prevent[ing] the French [from] settling on the Ohio." Dinwiddie also revealed his strategic thoughts on the region: "When three or four forts are properly finished, I think fifty men in each fort will be sufficient that will greatly encourage our friendly Indians." Dinwiddie also emphasized the insufficiency of the funding available in the Virginia Colony, pleading, "But as it is a National service, I am in hopes of assistance from Britain."[45]

Three days later, Dinwiddie responded to Washington with positive developments. Three sloops filled with recruits from the York and James River regions and Virginia's Eastern Shore would soon be on their way to join Washington. Regarding the uniforms Washington had requested, the lieutenant governor cautioned, "You have not time to get them made, unless to be sent after you." Concerned about funding for the expedition, Dinwiddie added, "Care should be taken of buying the cloth at the cheapest rate." Dinwiddie also enclosed Washington's commission as lieutenant colonel and informed him that George Muse had been appointed major. Muse had served with Lawrence Washington during the War of Jenkins' Ear and his deputy adjutant of the Middle Neck district of the Virginia Militia before rising to that position upon Lawrence's death in 1752.

In the larger scheme of the developing situation, Dinwiddie underestimated how quickly the French would reach the Forks of the Ohio. "I am surprised… that the French are so early expected down the Ohio, which I think makes

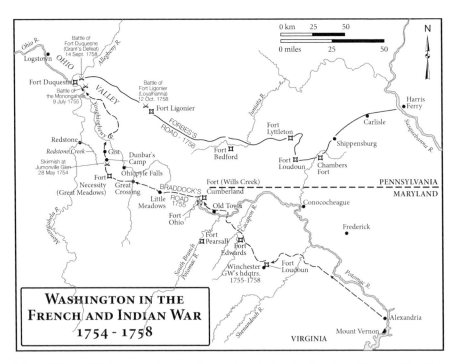

Map of George Washington's theater of operations during the French and Indian War. *Map by George Chakvetadze.*

it necessary for you to march what soldiers you have enlisted immediately to the Ohio & escort some wagons with the necessary provisions. Col. Fry [is] to march with the others as soon as possible." It would be more than two weeks before Washington was able to depart Alexandria, but Dinwiddie hoped "as Capt. Trent has begun to build a Fort at Allegheny [the Forks of the Ohio], that the French will not immediately disturb us there; and when our forces our properly collected we shall be able to keep possession and drive the French from the Ohio." In addition, the lieutenant governor reported that three independent companies of British Regulars would soon arrive to serve under Dinwiddie's command, at least as he envisioned it. In the end, only one company participated in the coming campaign. The militarily inexperienced Dinwiddie further hoped that the Cherokee and Catawba warriors from the Carolinas were already with Trent. They never arrived, and the French timetable upset Dinwiddie's hopes and plans.[46]

A grateful Washington received Dinwiddie's correspondence on March 20, expressing gratitude for his promotion to lieutenant colonel and committing to "adhere to all the proper Rules (as far as it is in my power) and discipline of the profession I have now entered into." He acknowledged, "I am vain enough to believe, I shall not be quite an unfit member for it [the army]." Little did he know just how long it would take to achieve success in his new profession. Washington had previously lobbied a member of the Virginia Council for the promotion. Washington did not seek overall command, "for I must be impartial enough to confess, it is a charge too great for my youth and inexperience." Instead, he desired the lieutenant colonelcy to learn under a "skillful commander or man of sense" and render himself "worthy of the promotion" that he had just received. That skillful commander proved to be Colonel Joshua Fry of Albemarle County. Since Washington's previous dispatch to Dinwiddie, the recruiting situation had improved even without the arrival of Dinwiddie's men. Washington had "about 75 men at Alexandria near 50 of which I have enlisted." The situation in the Valley looked better, too, as Captain Adam Stephen held his company in readiness to join forces with Washington at Winchester. On the logistics front, Major Carlisle prepared wagons and provisions. Nevertheless, concerns arose over the dearth of capable officers in the regiment, as two experienced men had declined commissions. Washington recommended his former interpreter Jacob Van Braam, "the oldest Lieutenant and an experienced soldier for a command." Washington's command was ill-prepared for their mission. Yet time was of the essence, and they soon embarked on their momentous journey to the Ohio Country.[47]

Dinwiddie clearly understood that Washington lacked military training and experience in making decisions under duress. Despite his inexperience, Washington possessed an abundance of ambition to become a British Regular officer and a strong desire to successfully serve Virginia and the Crown. He was a patriot who had "too sincere a love for my country" to undertake the mission in a manner that might jeopardize its success. He fully expected Colonel Fry to ultimately lead the way. Nevertheless, rapidly evolving circumstances in the field placed him at the helm of Dinwiddie's expedition. Washington's inexperience, ambition and eagerness to please his patron formed a volatile combination in the Ohio Country, where the French military was strengthening its own claims to the region. There, the tinder was dry, and all that was needed was a single spark to start a raging conflagration.

Chapter 3

"DESTINED TO MONONGAHELA"

Washington's March to the Ohio Country

At noon on Tuesday, April 2, 1754, Lieutenant Colonel George Washington marched his detachment out of Alexandria, Virginia. His command now numbered 160 officers and soldiers and one Swedish volunteer. Two wagons carrying supplies accompanied the expedition. In his later years, Washington proudly recalled departing "without waiting till the whole should be completed—or for a detachment from the Independent Companies of regulars." With his soldiers unaccustomed to the exertions of the march, the column covered only six miles that first day. Washington did not mention the hue of the men's coats, but the expedition was underway. They pitched their tents and spent the night at Cameron's Ordinary at the head of Hunting Creek.[48]

The route next took them to Quaker Edward Thompson's establishment near what became Hillsboro in Loudoun County. Washington's command ascended the Blue Ridge at Vestal's Gap on April 8 and crossed the Shenandoah River at John Vestal's ferry. Washington knew this country well, for he had surveyed much of it for Lord Fairfax and owned one thousand acres on Bullskin Run a few miles to the south. By April 18, Washington had reached Winchester, where he expected to find loaded supply wagons. They were not there, and supplies grew short, a soon to be common occurrence. "The difficulty in getting wagons has been insurmountable," he complained to Thomas Cresap at Oldtown on the Potomac. "We have found so much inconvenience attending it here in these roads that I am determined to carry all our provisions &c out on horseback." Washington asked Cresap

View of the South Branch of the Potomac River Valley from the Fort Pearsall site in Romney, West Virginia. *Author photo.*

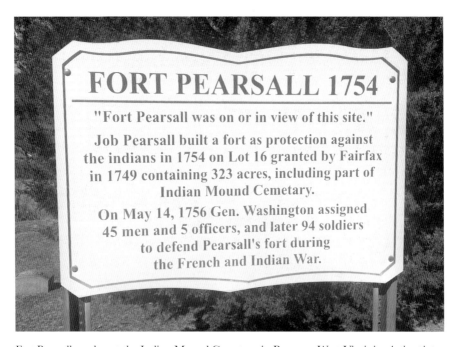

FORT PEARSALL 1754

"Fort Pearsall was on or in view of this site."

Job Pearsall built a fort as protection against the indians in 1754 on Lot 16 granted by Fairfax in 1749 containing 323 acres, including part of Indian Mound Cemetary.

On May 14, 1756 Gen. Washington assigned 45 men and 5 officers, and later 94 soldiers to defend Pearsall's fort during the French and Indian War.

Fort Pearsall marker at the Indian Mound Cemetery in Romney, West Virginia. *Author photo.*

to ready "kettles, tomahawks, best gun flints and axes from the [Ohio] Company Store," as well as all the flour he could obtain. On the bright side, Captain Adam Stephen's company of hardy Valley men met Washington at Winchester. Washington rode ahead of his command with a small party, riding through the hilly terrain west of town. On April 19, he arrived at Job Pearsall's Fort, a frontier home enclosed by a stockade near modern Romney, West Virginia.[49]

While waiting for the troops at Pearsall's, Washington received dire news. An express rider from Captain Trent at the Forks of the Ohio arrived, "demanding a reinforcement with all speed," as eight hundred French troops would soon arrive. Washington immediately informed Colonel Fry of the latest developments at the forks via a rider. Washington's trailing detachment arrived the following day, and he promptly rode seventeen miles northward along the old Shawnee Trail until he reached the North Branch of the Potomac River. He forded the stream and stopped on the north bank at Thomas Cresap's stockaded home overlooking the river. En route, Washington received more news that a massive French force had indeed descended the Ohio and captured Trent's fort.[50]

Site of Cresap's Fort at Oldtown, Maryland. *Author photo.*

Captain Trent received Dinwiddie's formal orders in early February 1754 while he was constructing a "strong Store House" for the Ohio Company situated on the Monongahela River at the Mouth of Redstone Creek near modern Brownsville, Pennsylvania. Trent wasted no time and dispatched couriers to several trading posts in the region, seeking additional recruits among the fur traders and frontiersmen. Although Dinwiddie had directed that Trent raise a company of one hundred men, he obtained fewer than half that number. Trent also notified the Iroquois leaders Tanaghrisson and Monacatoocha of the planned British actions.[51]

Trent quickly completed the storehouse and constructed rafts to ferry supplies downriver. The Half King urged him to hurry forward and build the fort at the forks. He also assured Trent that the chiefs would gather their people and assist him. With his small force, Trent headed for the forks. There he met Christopher Gist and George Croghan, whose half brother Ensign Edward Ward was an officer under Trent.

The construction began with the delivery of gifts to the Native Americans from Lieutenant Governor Dinwiddie and a speech by Trent to the Ohio Country Iroquois chiefs Tanaghrisson and Monacatoocha. Trent then "laid out the Fort and cleared the ground and got some logs squared." The Iroquois chiefs laid the first log of Trent's Fort and pledged to "make war against" anyone who interfere with its construction. For supplies, Trent possessed a large quantity of flour that he brought over the mountains during the dead of winter. The Indians in turn hunted and gave Trent meat for the groundbreaking ceremony. Trent also intended to trade with the local Delaware Indians. Ensign Ward reported that the Delawares "could not be prevailed up on to hunt tho' often applied to and offered great prices for any kind of meat they could bring in." The reluctance of the Delawares to trade with Trent was no surprise, as they "inclined to the French but were afraid to declare in their favor" in the presence the British. Trent's men lived predominately on the flour they brought, with an occasional hunted turkey. When that ran out, they subsisted on Indian corn. Unfortunately, Trent waited until the "corn and even salt to eat with it was scarce…and the weather so hot the men were not able to work having become very weak by having nothing but corn to eat."[52]

Morale at the forks plummeted. They unrealistically expected that Washington would have arrived by then with reinforcements and supplies. The Indians inclined to ally with the English became discouraged when they learned "how backward the Governor of Virginia was in sending troops." Trent's men had resided on the frontier, and the Indians did not consider them reinforcements from Virginia. Trent departed the forks in search of provisions, traveling as far as Fort Ohio on the Potomac. He found no provisions nor any sign of the Virginia Regiment. Trent obtained some rations from his nearby settlement and then headed back to the Forks of the Ohio.

George Croghan, serving as an interpreter for Trent, learned "from an Indian in the French Interest, [that] they might expect 400 French" down the Allegheny to the forks in thirteen days. Trent urged Washington to "march out to them with all possible Expedition." At the forks, Indians allied with the British informed Ward that Monsieur La Force warned them, "Neither they nor the English there, would see the Sun above 20 days longer." Seven of those days had already passed. On April 13, trader John Davison warned Ward of the approaching French force.[53]

With both Captain Trent and his second in command, Lieutenant John Frazier, the trader, away from the forks, Ward traveled eight miles upstream on the Monongahela River to Turtle Creek to Frazier's cabin. Ward explained the situation to Frazier. He did not doubt the imminent French arrival but simply replied, "What can we do in the affair?" The Half King and another Iroquois chief arrived the next morning, advising them to build a stockade. Ward requested Frazier to take command at the fort, but the trader declared that "he had a shilling to lose for a penny he should gain by his commission at that time." It would be six days at the earliest before Frazier could go to the forks. Although Ward's senior officers had abandoned him and departed without orders "how to proceed," he realized that the few Indians aligning themselves with the British were losing faith in their allies. Nevertheless, Ward returned to the forks and intended to "hold out to the last extremity before it should be said that the English had retreated like cowards before the French forces appeared."[54]

The French forces had a difficult journey to the forks amid the winter weather. Captain Claude-Pierre Pécaudy, Sieur de Contrecoeur, commandant of the French Fort Niagara, had assembled a large force of five hundred men composed of French Marines and Canadian militia to reinforce the outposts in the Ohio Country. The troops made an arduous journey through the wintry cold of Canada to reach Fort Niagara. The troops disrobed to cross ice-choked rivers and streams several times a day, holding their clothes and belongings overhead to keep them dry. Upon reaching the opposite bank, they quickly dressed and ran around to warm up. At Fort Niagara, many French troops ventured to visit the nearby falls, a breathtaking spectacle in its unaltered natural setting. Leaving the fort, they paddled canoes and bateaux along the southern shore of Lake Erie, battling the wintry winds to Fort Presque Isle (Erie, Pennsylvania), where they arrived on March 8. Contrecoeur's force then marched overland to Fort Le Boeuf, carrying the canoes and bateaux and dragging the artillery overland via portage. From Le Boeuf, they set out in their small vessels down French Creek to its junction with the Allegheny River at Fort Machault (modern Franklin, Pennsylvania). From there, they followed the Allegheny or la Belle Riviere to the Forks of the Ohio. On April 17, they spied the British building their fort.[55]

The large French flotilla numbering three hundred canoes and sixty bateaux containing seven hundred Frenchmen and nine cannons disembarked upstream from the British. Contrecoeur quickly ordered four cannons mounted on their carriages and marched toward the nascent British structure. Captain François LeMercier and a drummer advanced, demanding the British surrender their fort at 2:00 p.m. The French officer glanced at his watch and told Ward that he had one hour to decide and deliver it in writing to the French camp. The Half King advised Ward to tell the French that he had no authority to answer the French and request that they await Trent's return. The Iroquois chief "stormed greatly at the French at the time they were obliged to march out of the fort and told them it was he who ordered that Fort and laid the first log of it himself," but the French disregarded his words and ignored his antics. They had dealt with him before and knew that most Ohio Indians had lost confidence in him and were looking out for their own interest.[56]

Tanaghrisson had a previous fiery encounter with the French. In 1753, their fort building venture into the Ohio Country alarmed him and Monacatoocha. These Mingo sachems derived their authority over the local Shawnee and Delaware tribes as representatives of the Iroquois Nation's power from Onondaga, New York. The regional clout of the two leaders was tenuous, and the encroachment of both the French and British threatened the Iroquois's delicate balance of power over the Delawares and Shawnees, who grew weary of Iroquois dominance. That summer, at a conference for the purpose of strengthening ties between the Virginians and the Ohio Indians, Tanaghrisson declared that he would "warn the French off our land."[57]

In September 1753, he ventured to Fort Presque Isle and confronted the French commander, Captain Pierre Paul de La Malgue, Sieur de Marin. "The river where we are belongs to us warriors," proclaimed Tanaghrisson, "the chiefs who look after affairs [i.e., the Onondaga Council] are not its

Tanaghrisson, the Iroquois Half King, as depicted at the Fort Necessity National Battlefield Visitor Center. *Author photo.*

masters. It is a good road for warriors and not their chiefs." He asked Marin what the French intentions were "so that we can calm down our wives." The Half King next presented Marin a wampum belt that signaled the French to halt their advance and fort building expedition. "This is the first and last demand we shall make of you, and I shall strike at whoever does not listen to us," threatened the Half King. "You seem to have lost your minds," retorted Marin as he rejected the wampum. "I despise all the stupid things you said. I know that they come only from you, and that all the warriors and chiefs of the Belle Riviere think better than you and take pity on their women and children." The next day, a Shawnee delegation met the French and "distanced themselves from Tanaghrisson's hard line." He departed Fort Presque Isle a humiliated man, and the French realized that the Ohio tribes rejected his leadership. When the French seized the forks in 1754, his humiliation was doubled.[58]

At the designated time, Ward, the Half King and three soldiers went to the French camp, where they met Contrecoeur. Ward proceeded as Half King advised, but the French captain rejected his plea, demanding an answer. If not, they would take the fort by force. Ward assessed the situation, with seven hundred French troops and "several pieces of artillery pointed at the fort within musket shot." With only forty-one soldiers, workmen and "travelers who happened to be there at the time," Ward prudently surrendered Fort Prince George. He dined with the French officers, who quizzed him on British politics, of which he knew nothing. Contrecoeur offered to buy the carpentry tools in Ward's camp, but the ensign retorted, "I love my King and Country too well to part with any of them." The next morning, Ward led his detachment to the Ohio Company storehouse on the Redstone and then on to Wills Creek, where he met Lieutenant Colonel Washington. Meanwhile, the French quickly constructed Fort Duquesne at the Forks of the Ohio.[59]

Ward explained the developments to Washington and presented him a speech from the Half King, asking "if you are ready to come." Two young Mingo warriors arrived with Ward to serve as messengers. Eager to take vengeance on the French, Tanaghrisson wrote, "We are now ready to fall upon them, waiting only for your succor. Have good courage and come as soon as possible; you will find us ready to encounter with them as you are yourselves." Although Tanaghrisson was a willing ally, he controlled a very small group of warriors and their families, and their numbers paled in comparison to the Native Americans who quickly gravitated toward the French. Washington did not understand the reality of the situation with the Ohio Country Indians and frequently accepted the Half King's assertions and advice to the Virginian's own detriment.[60]

Ward's arrival at Wills Creek confirmed the reports that Washington had received and eliminated any doubt about the situation at the forks. Examining Washington's orders from Lieutenant Governor Dinwiddie and the applicability to the current situation, the French had certainly obstructed the British construction of their fort at the forks using military force. Now Washington had to act; Dinwiddie had directed that such offenders are to be "restrained." If the offending French resisted the attempted restraint, Washington was authorized "to make prisoners of or kill & destroy them." Dinwiddie likely assumed that Washington would be at the forks before the French arrived there. However, time had rendered the initial orders moot. Instead, Washington found himself in a situation where he would have to rely on his own judgment. "For the rest," wrote Dinwiddie, "you are to conduct yourself as the circumstances of the service shall require, & act as

Artistic rendition of the French and Indians at Fort Duquesne, located in the Allegheny County Courthouse, Pittsburgh, Pennsylvania. *Author photo.*

you shall find best for the furtherance of His Majesty's service, & and the good of his dominion." The time had come for Washington to make his first critical command decision as military a leader.[61]

On April 23, Washington called a council of war at Fort Ohio, on the Virginia shore of the Potomac River, opposite Wills Creek. Based on various sources, his council consisted of the officers of Washington's detachment from the Virginia Regiment. He outlined the situation and presented the speeches of Half King and the other Mingo chiefs. Trent had informed Washington that the French numbered 1,000 men with eighteen artillery pieces. Although much exaggerated, the French nevertheless numbered many hundreds more than Washington had. He explained that his force numbered only 150 men, and Trent had 33 soldiers. Washington concluded that he obviously lacked sufficient force to attack the French.[62]

Although outnumbered, the young commander determined to push ahead to the Ohio Company blockhouse at the confluence of Redstone Creek with the Monongahela River "about thirty-seven miles this side of the [French] fort." Washington intended to clear a road through the virgin

Above: The Forks of the Ohio and site of Fort Duquesne at the Point State Parking, looking straight ahead toward the Ohio River formed by the Monongahela flowing in from the left and joining the Allegheny River entering from the right. *Author photo.*

Opposite, top: Site of Fort Ohio in Ridgely, West Virginia, where Washington conducted a council of war upon learning of the French capture of forks of the Ohio from Ensign Ward's party. *Author photo.*

Opposite, bottom: Fort Ohio Historic Marker in Ridgely, West Virginia, across the Potomac River from Cumberland, Maryland. *Author photo.*

woodlands from Wills Creek to Redstone to facilitate the passage of artillery and wagons that would follow him. The storehouse at Redstone already contained provisions from the Ohio Company, and he would improve the works begun by Trent earlier in the year. Washington believed that his presence in the region, while insufficient to challenge the French at Fort Duquesne, would lift the spirits of British settlers, traders and frontiersmen and "encourage the *Indians* our allies, to remain in our interest." Washington viewed his advance as the establishment of a bridgehead in the Ohio Country on which arriving reinforcements could organize for action against the French at the forks. Based on Dinwiddie's plans, Washington expected as many as seven hundred men to follow in several detachments.[63]

After deciding on a course of action, Washington communicated news of the developments in the Ohio Country and his planned action to the Pennsylvania and Maryland governors. He thought it "advisable to acquaint your honor of it immediately than wait 'till you could get intelligence by way of Williamsburg." Washington reported "credible accounts" of a party of the French coming up the Ohio from Venango, as well as six hundred Chippewas and Ottawas moving to reinforce Fort Duquesne. Washington emphasized "that the Indians [Tanaghrisson] expect some assistance from you, and I am persuaded you will take notice of their moving speech and of their unshaken fidelity."[64]

The next day, Washington sent Ensign Ward to Williamsburg. Emphasizing the urgency of this duty, Washington provided his own horse and equestrian accoutrements to Ward. He carried a letter from Washington on the situation and copies of the letters to the other governors, although the ensign would certainly be queried by Dinwiddie and provide more detailed information. One of the Mingo warriors accompanied Ward to "be an eyewitness" to Virginia's preparations to support them and formally present Tanaghrisson's wampum and speech to Dinwiddie. In the report to Dinwiddie, Washington's explained his next steps:[65]

> *I am destined to Monongahela with all the diligent dispatch in my power. We will endeavor to make the road sufficiently good for the heaviest artillery to pass and when we arrive at Redstone Creek fortified ourselves as strongly as the short time will allow of. I doubt not but to maintain a possession there till we are reinforced (if it seasonably arrives) unless the waters rising admit their cannon to be conveyed up in canoes and then I flatter myself we shall not be so wanting for intelligence but to get timely notice of it and make a good retreat.*[66]

On April 25, Washington initiated his westward trek by sending sixty soldiers forward to "make and amend the road."[67]

On May 4 in Williamsburg, Ward, the Mingo warrior and an interpreter entered the Virginia Governor's Palace and appeared before the Virginia Council. The rugged group from the frontier surely presented quite a spectacle to the prim and proper power brokers in Virginia's colonial capital. Ward explained the French seizure of Fort Prince George and the incidents that preceded it. He also delivered Washington's letters and the Half King's speech and wampum, as well as the original copy of the French summons to Dinwiddie. When Trent informed Dinwiddie of the circumstances of the fall of Fort Prince George, the lieutenant governor raged at the conduct of Trent and Frazier. He sent orders to Colonel Fry to "try them by court martial." Dinwiddie hoped that they would receive "such punishment as the unaccountable action deserves."[68]

The French seizure of the initiative set Dinwiddie into a flurry of action as his plans spiraled out of control and became obsolete. He wrote to the Earl of Holderness, calling the French belligerence at the forks an "extraordinary step." With such naked aggression against Virginia, Dinwiddie let it be known that he "ordered the Forces raised in this Dominion and those raised in North Carolina to march to Redstone Creek" thirty-five miles south of the forks. An Independent Company of British Regulars from South Carolina that had just arrived in Williamsburg would soon join them.[69]

The lieutenant governor also notified the Lords of the Treasury and Trade in London. "I am now endeavoring to collect together all the Forces I can… to dislodge them from the King's Fort."[70] He forwarded a copy of the French commander's summons to surrender, which Dinwiddie considered "to be a most egregious Violation of the Treaties subsisting between the two Crowns."[71] A dispatch to the Earl of Halifax revealed the level of his passion. He declared, "It will grieve me to allow the French a Quiet Settlement on the Ohio, as I foresee the Inconveniency, and I may say, ruin to all His Majesty's Colonies on this Continent." For all of Dinwiddie's fury, the other colonial governors did not share his level of concern. Some believed that he was acting more on behalf of the Ohio Company than the Crown. In fact, it might be argued that the developing conflict could be known as Governor Dinwiddie's War.[72]

On May 4, Dinwiddie told Washington that his reinforcements had "been delayed by unfortunate circumstances." Washington quickly learned that in war, plans frequently unraveled. On the plus side, the Independent Company of British Regulars from South Carolina had arrived in Williamsburg and would depart for Alexandria and the Ohio Country. Two additional Independent Companies from New York were expected in ten days. A regiment of North Carolina militia under Colonel James Innes "are imagined to be on their march." Of these, only the South Carolina company would reach Washington in time to be of assistance. Even Colonel Fry with the balance of the Virginia Regiment was delayed, much to Dinwiddie's surprise. So much for Washington learning from a senior and experienced gentleman—Fry could have learned a thing or two from the younger officer about urgency.[73]

By May 9, Washington had reached Little Meadows, about twenty miles west of Wills Creek. He had not yet received Dinwiddie's latest missive on reinforcements, but he informed the governor of his supply problems. If Trent were not already in enough trouble with Dinwiddie, Washington's letter did him no favors. Washington expressed disappointment that Trent failed to provide sufficient packhorses, as his communications to Major Carlyle and Washington indicated he would. "There was none in readiness, nor any in expectation that I would receive," complained the young Virginian. Now Washington waited while wagons and teams were gathered from among the more numerous settlers of the South Branch of the Potomac River Valley, south of Wills Creek in Virginia.[74]

At Little Meadows, Washington had received several reports from British traders abandoning the Ohio Country due to the French presence at the forks. Estimates of French strength ranged to 600 at Fort Duquesne, with 800 more en route. Either way, Washington could not match French firepower with his 160 men. He also learned that Monsieur La Force's scouts were fanning out over the frontier and gathering up information on the English approach. Washington followed suit, sending Captain Adam Stephen and 25 men to Gist's Plantation on the western edge of the mountains just north of what is now Uniontown, Pennsylvania. Washington instructed Stephen to query the inhabitants about the location of La Force and his detachment. If they were nearby, Washington directed Stephen to cease pursuit and look out for the safety of his command. However, if they could find any Frenchman isolated from his command, then Stephen should "seize him and bring him to us that we might learn what we could from him." Washington was also eager to learn "if there was any possibility" of using the Youghiogheny River and Redstone Creek to reach the Ohio Company blockhouse on the Monongahela.[75]

Carrying four days of provisions, Stephen dispatched hunters for meat, while the rest of the men labored to make rafts. Heavy rains had swelled the mountain streams, making crossings difficult. Stephen passed Gist's Plantation and followed Redstone Creek to the Monongahela River. There, English traders, "whom the French had permitted to retire," informed Stephen that a French scouting detachment had returned to Fort Duquesne due to the heavy rains. Stephen paid "a person," perhaps a trader or frontiersman, to gather intelligence about the French. Five days later, he returned with "the most satisfactory and accurate account of everything at Fort Duquesne." Having paid the "fellow" five pounds for the scout, Stephen concluded that the French had likely paid him for equally accurate information on the Virginians at Redstone. So, they quickly gathered their belongings and rejoined Washington.[76]

Meanwhile, Washington and his men filed out of their bivouac at Little Meadows on May 12. The rains swelled the Casselman River, which the men forded in water "up to their arm-pits." Although they barely covered three miles, Washington encamped his troops on high ground "to dry ourselves." Good news arrived with an express rider informing Washington that Fry was at Winchester with 100 men and soon would join Washington. Even better, Colonel James Innes with 350 North Carolinians was on his way, and Maryland had committed to raise 200 men for the campaign. Surprisingly, recalcitrant Pennsylvania, "as the province that furnished no recruits," committed £10,000 "to pay the soldiers raised in other colonies." In New England, Massachusetts planned a raid on Canada with 600 men to divert French attention from the Ohio Country. In the end, none of these came to fruition except for the arrival of Fry's detachment of the Virginia Regiment. At the time it was received, however, the news surely buoyed Washington's spirits and gave his effort to establish a lodgment at Redstone more relevance.[77]

By May 17, Washington had arrived at the Great Crossing of the Youghiogheny River. He halted here for several days, as the rain-swollen waters prevented the wagons carrying provisions from crossing. Ensign Ward and the Indian who had gone to Williamsburg returned to Washington that evening, bringing Dinwiddie's communication of May 4. The Indian promptly departed to update the Half King on Washington's progress and plans. Dinwiddie endorsed Washington's plan to advance to the mouth of Redstone Creek on the Monongahela River and directed Colonel Fry to rendezvous there with Washington.

Washington replied immediately, notifying the lieutenant governor that Indians from the Ohio reported that eight hundred French reinforcements were expected at Fort Duquesne, the newly constructed French fort at the Forks of the Ohio. Washington proudly noted that the French located their fortress where Washington had suggested in his 1753 voyage to deliver Dinwiddie's summons to the French. Their scouts also penetrated "within 6 or 7 miles of our camp" and evaded detection. Furthermore, the men of Trent's company were creating problems in the camp by "their refractory behavior." To avoid dissension spreading to the men of the Virginia Regiment, Washington separated Trent's command and ordered them to Fort Ohio at Wills Creek to await orders from Dinwiddie.[78]

Washington wrote a second dispatch to Dinwiddie on May 18, complaining about command issues. It was an immature and unprofessional action to take during a military campaign. Washington and his officers had drawn up a list of complaints, chief among them being the pay scale that the Virginia Assembly had set for the expedition to the Ohio. The trouble had begun earlier in May, when the officers of the Virginia Regiment learned that Trent's company had been enlisted at a higher rate of pay. Furthermore, pay in the British army was higher than that which "his majesty's subjects in Virginia" were permitted. Many officers were prepared to resign over the matter, so Washington took up the cudgel on their behalf as well as his own.

In his missive to Dinwiddie, Washington declared that he was "heartily concerned" about the officers' complaints, "and still more to find my inclinations prone to second their just grievances." He noted that despite their grievances, their honor would not allow them to resign with "the approaching danger." Instead, they remained in the service until changes could be made offering "their best endeavors voluntarily."[79] More important than the officers' quibbles, Washington expressed dismay over the expedition due to "so many clogs" and noted, "I quite despair of success." However, he assured Dinwiddie that he would not resign his commission, but rather "humbly begged" to continue in service as a volunteer lieutenant colonel than "to be slaving dangerously for the shadow of pay, through woods, rocks, and mountains."[80]

Dinwiddie received this letter when he arrived in Winchester for a tentative conference with Indian leaders and promptly lashed out at Washington on May 25. "I am concerned and no less surprised to find your letter of the 18th of the month, such ill-timed complaints and sorry to find you think they are." Dinwiddie pointed out that the officers should have raised the pay issue at the time of enlistment. They "knew well the terms on which they were to serve and were satisfied then with it." Dinwiddie also pointed out that "the hardships complained of…are such as usually attend on a Military Life and are considered by Soldiers rather as opportunities of Glory than objects of Discouragement," a comment that surely stung Washington with his military aspirations. Dinwiddie pointed out that he had received "no complaints of this kind from Colonel Fry or his corps, and I hope that you will take care not to let them know anything of your dissatisfaction—communicate the above to your officers." But Dinwiddie was not finished; he had only addressed the complaints of the officers. Now he addressed Washington's personal behavior in the matter.

Washington's letter had caught Dinwiddie off guard. After all, the governor had given the inexperienced Washington high rank in an important military campaign, and now the young man seemingly disregarded the favor he had been shown. His complaints caused Dinwiddie much concern, coming as they were from "a Gentleman whom

I so particularly considered, and from whom I had so great expectations and hopes." The letter dumbfounded the governor, who believed that its author "appear[ed] so differently from himself and give me leave to say mistakenly as I think, concurring with complaints in general so ill founded." Washington's actions so alarmed Dinwiddie that he wrote to Fry, warning him, "I expect you [to] communicate your affairs only to me, and that you do so regularly as occasion requires." He added, "I conceive there is some discontent crept into the detachment under Colo. Washington." Although the governor considered the issues "not well founded," he ordered Fry "to prevent so dangerous an Evil from spreading among them (but without letting it be known that I have mentioned it to you)." "Touch on this tender point with great discretion," Dinwiddie advised.[81]

Fortunately, Washington had not yet received the stinging reply and embarked none the wiser by canoe to explore the Youghiogheny and evaluate its potential as transportation route. He departed the Great Crossing on May 20 with a lieutenant, three soldiers and one Native American warrior. They paddled downstream for a half mile, and then he went ashore to confer with a trader, who discouraged Washington from seeking a water route. Washington disregarded the advice and continued in the canoe, while the others waded in the shallow water, reaching Turkey-Foot, now the village of Confluence, roughly eight miles from the Great Crossing. Washington surveyed the area about Turkey-Foot and "found it very convenient to build a Fort." The location was gravelly and situated at the confluence of three small rivers. Ever the surveyor, Washington drew up a plan for a potential fort before continuing his journey down the Youghiogheny. The Indian unexpectedly refused to proceed any farther until Washington gifted him a ruffled shirt, which the colonel supplied from his personal effects.[82]

They discovered the Youghiogheny to be rock filled, with many differing currents. Although the churning waters swollen from recent rains, they easily waded through. They encountered shallow runs where the water flowed rapidly with steep mountains on both banks. About ten miles downstream from Turkey-Foot, the river "became so rapid as to oblige us to come ashore." At last, he came to the falls at what is now called Ohiopyle and realized that his search for a water route to the Monongahela was in vain, just as the trader had advised. Returning to Great Crossing on May 23, he wrote to Fry, "This day I returned from my discoveries down the Youghiogheny, which, I am sorry to say, can never be made navigable. We traced the watercourse nearly thirty miles, with the full expectation of succeeding in the much-desired aim; but, at length, we came to a fall, which continued rough, rocky

Ohiopyle Falls and its associated rapids on the Youghiqheny River prevented Washington from using a water route to the Monongahela. *Author photo.*

and scarcely passable for two miles, then fell, within the space of fifty yards, nearly forty feet perpendicular."[83]

Washington shared much information with Fry as well. The latest intelligence placed seven hundred to eight hundred Frenchmen at Fort Duquesne, but rumors swirled that half the force had been sent on "some secret expedition." He also suggested that Fry request "treaty goods" or bribes for the Indians who assist them. One Native American told Washington, "The French always had Indians to show them the woods, because they paid well for so doing." Washington suggested that the English should abide by the same maxim to keep the Indians satisfied.[84]

Chapter 4

"I HEARD THE BULLETS WHISTLE"

The Battle of Jumonville Glen

In May 1754, Washington's force was operating outside an exclusionary zone that French governor Duquesne declared "Incontestable Territory." While His Most Christian Majesty King Louis the XV of France had ordered Duquesne to seize the forks of la Belle Riviere, the exact boundaries of that territory remained vague. In April 1754, Governor Duquesne established approximate boundaries at thirty to thirty-six miles from the river. He advised Captain Contrecoeur, the commander of French forces at the Forks of the Ohio, "I would not take exception to what they [the British] might build at a distance from the Belle River....I would certainly not pick a quarrel with people who would be 10 to 12 leagues distant from the riverbank." However, tension grew at Fort Duquesne when French-allied Indians informed Contrecoeur that Washington's force was en route and "coming armed with overt force." With Captain Stephen's detachment venturing west to the Monongahela River, a tributary of the Ohio or Belle River, it would not be long before the French acted.[85]

On May 23, Captain Contrecoeur dispatched Ensign Joseph Coulon de Villiers, Sieur de Jumonville, to track down the English and determine if they were on French lands. The thirty-five-year-old Jumonville was born in 1718 the son of Nicolas-Antoine Coulon de Villiers, a French nobleman who came to New France as an officer in the Troupes de la Marine around 1700. His father attained a lofty record of combat experience, rising to the rank of captain, the highest attainable in the French Marines, and fought until he was killed in battle in 1733. Five of Nicolas-Antoine's sons followed their father as officers in the Marine companies, with the three eldest becoming accomplished officers. Joseph, the second youngest, lacked their renown, but he had seen combat, including fighting alongside his father and brothers against the Fox and Sauk Indians at La Baye (modern Green Bay, Wisconsin). In heated combat, the Indians killed his father, one brother and a brother-in-law, besides wounding another brother, Louis Coulon de Villiers. Joseph also participated in the Chickasaw War at Tupelo in 1739–40 and King George's War, where he led a raiding party against the English in 1748. Despite this experience, his career, as biographer Joseph L. Peyser wrote, "was slow in developing." Nevertheless, his experience significantly exceeded that of his opponent, George Washington.[86]

If the English were discovered on French-claimed land, Jumonville was to deliver a summons ordering them away. When he found them, Contrecoeur further directed Jumonville "to send us a good pair of legs in order to inform us about what he has learned on the day he expects to make the summons." Jumonville's party included the officers Pierre Jacques Druillon de Mace and commissary and Indian interpreter and expert Michal Pepin de La Force, two cadets and thirty-one soldiers. They departed Fort Duquesne on May 23 in pirogues, canoes made from hollowed-out tree trunks, rowing up the Monongahela until they came to the "shed," as the French referred to the Ohio Company blockhouse on Redstone Creek. From there, they moved eastward over the hilly, rolling countryside of what is now Fayette County, Pennsylvania, toward the mountains where Washington's force lay. Jumonville's actions during this time are sketchy, and details remain elusive. They encountered local Indians, perhaps Mingos. Jumonville, and likely La Force, pleaded with the Indians to lead them to the English camp so that the French could learn of Washington's intentions, "but none of them could be prevailed on to be our guides." Eventually, Jumonville's party visited Gist's settlement and began to pillage it, but two Indians whom Gist had posted as guards dissuaded the French from molesting the property. They then ascended the mountains and encamped in a rocky hollow on May 26, concealed deep in the woods a half mile from the nearest woodland trace. Inundated by rain, they constructed crude log and bark huts for shelter. Jumonville also sent scouts out to explore the area and locate Washington's encampment.[87]

Jumonville's departure did not go unnoticed, with the seemingly ever-present Half King and his Mingo band in the area. Early on May 24, he sent Washington an exaggerated warning that "the French Army is set out to meet M. *George Washington.*" As previously planned, the Virginians departed their encampment at the Great Crossing early that morning and marched

A French soldier, as depicted at the Fort Necessity National Battlefield Visitor Center. *Author photo.*

twelve miles west to Great Meadow, a lush grassland oasis in the wilds of the highland forests. Washington's command reached the meadows at 2:00 p.m., and before long, an English trader entered the nascent bivouac and told Washington that he had seen two Frenchmen at Gist's Plantation the previous night. Furthermore, he noted that a strong French detachment was lurking in the area, confirming the Half King's warning. Washington surveyed the meadow with an eye toward establishing a defensive position and noticed clear waters rippling through two streams bisecting the field. From his raw military perspective, Washington deemed them "two natural intrenchments," behind which he placed his troops and wagons. On the next day, Washington dispatched several small scouting parties into the dark forests in search of the Frenchmen. He also mounted a squad of soldiers on draft horses and sent them out to range deeper into the territory ahead "to examine the Country well, and endeavor to get some News of the French." None of the scouting detachments located any French, leaving Washington bereft of intelligence on his enemy's whereabouts, but that was about to change.[88]

Early on the morning of May 27, Christopher Gist rode into Washington's encampment at Great Meadows and reported that Monsieur La Force and fifty men visited his settlement the previous day. After two Native American guards stopped them from killing a cow and pillaging, the French asked for the Half King. Gist also revealed that he had seen the tracks of the French within five miles of Great Meadows. After hearing this, Washington immediately detailed Captain Peter Hogg, Lieutenant George Mercer and Ensign William La Peronie with seventy-two men to track the French party. This constituted nearly half of Washington's entire force, so he must have placed confidence in Gist's information. Presumably, Hogg's detachment marched in the general direction of Gist's settlement, which would have taken them past the concealed French. Washington also cunningly told the Mingos in his camp that the French "wanted to kill the Half King," who was encamped about six miles west of the Great Meadow and not far from Jumonville's concealed camp. The supposed French threats to Tanaghrisson stoked the combative fires in the young warriors, and they eagerly volunteered to assist in tracking the French and carried the news to the Half King. One young warrior raced through the damp woods and warned the Half King of the French presence. Washington hoped to "incite their warriors to fall upon" the French.[89]

Meanwhile, Tanaghrisson had not been idle; his hatred of the French needed little motivation to spur him to action. In fact, Washington's desire to cross swords with the Canadians played right into the Half King's hands, escalating the strife between the two great European powers in North America. His warriors had discovered tracks on the muddy woodland trail and followed them to "a low obscure place," where the chief concluded the French were encamped. He dispatched Washington a messenger with the developing information. At 8:00 p.m., the rain-soaked Mingo runner dashed into the Great Meadow encampment and excitedly told Washington that the Half King was confident that the French were encamped near the Indians' bivouac. Washington had heard nothing from Captain Hogg's detachment, which had likely marched within half a mile of the secluded French camp. Hogg already had nearly half of Washington's force with him, leaving the commander bereft of manpower. Nevertheless, he determined that the opportunity to capture La Force, the presumed French commander, and his force could not be passed up. Washington detailed thirty men to stand guard at Great Meadow to protect the ammunition and supplies in the event the French attacked.[90]

Then he rushed out with forty men toward Tanaghrisson's camp, located a little more than four miles westward at a natural rock outcropping immortalized as the Half King's Rock. Washington led his men hurriedly through "a heavy rain and in a night as dark as pitch" along a narrow path through the dank woodlands. Men crowded into one another in the darkness and stumbled. Amid the blackness of night and the downpour of rain, they struggled to keep their ammunition dry moving through the woods. Finally, at sunrise, Washington and his drenched Virginians reached the large rocks on Chestnut Ridge where the Half King and his small band camped.[91]

There the leaders conferred with differing motivations, perceptions of the situation and who was in charge. Both men saw each other as an adjunct to their objectives and designs. For Washington, the French had forcibly taken the English fort at the Forks of the Ohio in April under threat of military violence and compulsorily driven English traders from the Ohio Country. Furthermore, given the strong language of Dinwiddie's orders, Washington undoubtedly felt justified in acting against the French party that had also just raided Gist's British settlement. In the young Virginian's mind and in accordance with his orders, a state of war, brought on by the French actions, already existed in the Ohio Country. For Washington, now was the time "to restrain all such Offenders, and in Case of resistance to make Prisoners of or kill & destroy them." From Tanaghrisson's standpoint, the French refusal to take his demands seriously and disregard of his purported leadership of all Ohio Indians was a personal affront to his honor. This plus his belief that the French had killed his father combined to inflame a passion to exact

The Half King's Rock, located about 1.5 miles south of Jumonville Glen. Here the Half King Tanaghrisson encamped with his small band. Washington joined him early on May 28, 1754, and the two men jointly planned their surprise attack on Jumonville's party at this location and returned here afterward. *Author photo.*

vengeance from the French. Despite differing motivations and perceptions, they both shared the common goal of defeating the French designs in the Ohio Country. Each man probably perceived himself the leader of the coming action, although the younger Washington was deferential to the Half King's age and experience. United by the common objective of striking the French interlopers, they quickly agreed "to go hand in hand and strike the French."[92]

By the early light of sunrise, the party of slightly less than forty Virginians and twelve Mingo warriors of the great Iroquois Nation moved without hesitation toward the French encampment. Although the rain had ceased, droplets of water fell from the leaves above as the war party moved through the dank forest. They followed a trail or narrowly hewn road that eventually wound its way several miles down the mountain toward Gist's settlement. After proceeding only half a mile from the rock, they halted while two Indian scouts followed the tracks of the French into the woods to the east and reconnoitered the French dispositions. The scouts discovered the French encamped at the base of a steep glen with a nearly perpendicular rock escarpment on the glen's western edge. Commanding hills sheltered the camp to the south and east. A wet weather stream flowed northward from the ravine, offering the only ready means of entrance or escape. Now that the French had been discovered, the concealed encampment became a trap.

The scouts quickly returned and explained the French dispositions to Tanaghrisson and Washington. Given that Washington knew little of their language and later complained about the lack of an interpreter, he probably found himself reliant on the Indians at this critical moment. The experienced Native American leaders, Tanaghrisson and Monacatoocha, grasped the mantle of command as the force moved out to attack Jumonville's command. They surveyed the ground and took control of tactical dispositions, showing Washington where to position his men on the high ground to the west and south overlooking the French position. Washington reported, "I in

Jumonville Glen, scene of the French camp in the low ground where Washington and the Half King launched a surprise attack against Ensign Jumonville's small force early on the morning of May 28, 1754. From atop the rock ledge, Captain Adam Stephen's Virginians fired into the French, while Washington charged in from an area to the lower left well out of the view of this picture. *Author photo.*

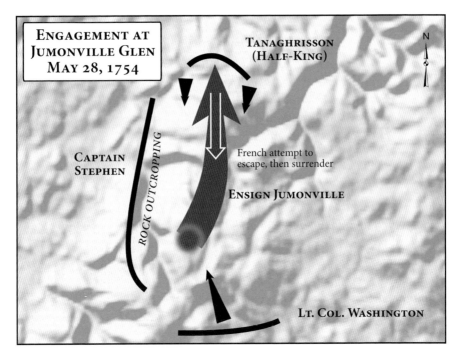

Battle of Jumonville Glen map, based on a National Park Service interpretive marker. *Map by George Chakvetadze.*

conjunction with the Half King and Monacatoocha, formed a disposition to attack them on all sides." Tanaghrisson led nine warriors to the left (north) and blocked the only potential escape route for the French troops. Monacatoocha and a young warrior named Cherokee Jack swung around to the far right (east), sealing the French in the glen.[93]

When Washington led the Virginians into their combat positions, they numbered only thirty-three soldiers, with several men having lost their way during the night march. Washington placed Captain Adam Stephen's company atop the rocky precipice overlooking the glen. He then led Lieutenant Waggener's company to the hill on the right and advanced downhill toward the French.[94]

The arrival of the Native Americans and the Virginians found the French at breakfast, sometime between seven and eight o'clock in the morning on May 28, 1754. The French troops milled about their camp, preparing breakfast and readying for the day, completely unaware of the fury about to unleashed on them. Some might have still been asleep. As Washington advanced his wing toward the French, a cracking branch or some other noise

Washington's Virginians deploying to attack the French at Jumonville Glen, May 28, 1754. *Author photo.*

alerted the French to the approaching threat. They scrambled and grabbed their Charleville muskets. According to some sources, one of the Frenchmen fired at the approaching Virginians, initiating the firefight. Other sources claimed that the Virginians fired first. One Native American account even stated that Washington personally fired the first shot as a signal to begin the attack. Washington acknowledged ordering his men to fire. Regardless of who fired the first shot, Washington and Tanaghrisson were certainly engaged in an offensive operation against Jumonville's command when the gunfire erupted, and their actions initiated the engagement.[95]

Although some of the Virginians' muskets failed to discharge owing to the wet weather, several French were struck with the opening volley. The French Marines returned fire at the Virginians in Washington's wing, killing one and wounding a few others, including Waggener. Bullets zipped past Lieutenant Colonel Washington, prompting him tell his younger brother Jack, "The right wing, where I stood, was exposed to and received all the enemy's fire....I heard the bullets whistle, and, believe me, there is something charming in the sound." This quote later made its way to King George II,

A Virginian firing from behind the rocks at Jumonville Glen, as portrayed at the Fort Necessity National Battlefield Visitor Center. *Author photo.*

the last British monarch to lead troops in battle. He quipped, "He would not say so if he had been used to hear many."[96]

Atop the high escarpment, Stephen's Virginians fired a ragged volley from their moist muskets, and he then ordered them to fix bayonets. His Virginians carefully worked their way around and down the rock-strewn descent from the heights. Meanwhile, Washington's men continued to fire at the confused French contingent, hitting "seven or eight." Surprised and stunned by the suddenness of the attack, the French ran toward the soggy low ground at the northern end of the glen. They did not get far before the Half King and his warriors emitted a ferocious battle cry and charged at the unsuspecting French, killing five of them. The French stopped, and La Force realized that his men "were all likely to lose their lives under the hands of the savages, called to his men, and immediately, with great precipitation, ran towards the English, flung down their arms, and begged for quarter." La Force saw Monacatoocha, whom he had known previously, near Washington and quickly surrendered to him. Most French followed suit and threw down their arms, surrendering to Washington and his men. Ensign Druillon surrendered to Captain Stephen.[97]

After stopping to scalp the French the Indians had killed and wounded, Tanaghrisson and his band followed the fleeing Canadians toward Washington. The Half King raised his tomahawk at La Force, but Washington intervened, saving him from a gory fate. Jumonville did not share his good fortune. The wounded French commander had been sitting on the ground, imploring Washington to cease firing through an interpreter, when the French fled at Washington's initial onset. The interpreter excitedly explained in the confusing situation that Jumonville was on a diplomatic mission. He did not have long to make his case, as Tanaghrisson approached and eyed up Jumonville. "Tu n'es pas encore mort, mon pere," meaning "You are not yet dead, my father," declared the chief. The Half King then raised his tomahawk and swung several mighty blows on the wounded officer's head, splitting it open. Then, in a display of gore that surely stunned Washington, his Virginians and the onlooking French, Tanaghrisson grabbed Jumonville's brain, yanked it from his skull and smashed it in his bare hands. Onlooking soldiers thought that the Iroquois chief had washed his hands with the Frenchman's brain. The other Native Americans took his cue and wielded their knives with ghastly dexterity, killing and scalping all the French wounded before Washington regained control of the situation.[98]

Druillon and La Force sought physical security behind Washington, who shielded them from Jumonville's fate. Tanaghrisson and his braves attempted to kill more of the French so they could take their scalps. Washington, "with great difficulty," prevented the Indians from "doing them further mischief." The Half King raged that all the French needed to be scalped, as it was the Indian way of fighting, and the warriors must have scalps. Furthermore, it needed to be done to avenge the death of his father at the hands of the French. With much anguish, Washington convinced him to be satisfied with the scalps that they had already taken.[99]

The sight of a dozen dead and dying Frenchmen bloodily relieved of their scalps by the Half King and his warriors must have presented a macabre spectacle for the Virginians. Inexperienced at war, they knew not the horrors of a battlefield, but now they had seen human cruelty up close and personal. Washington never admitted it or perhaps even realized it as it was occurring, but the situation had spiraled beyond his control as both he and the Half King led their men to the attack with completely different understandings of what was about to occur. Left to his own devices, Washington probably would have rendered aid to the wounded Jumonville when the combat ceased, keeping with European military tradition. Nevertheless, the fifteen-minute fight at Jumonville Glen soon turned into an international incident, and Washington as the senior English officer on the scene might as well have personally killed the French commander. It was later written that the "volley fired by a young Virginian in the backwoods of America set the world on fire."[100]

With the Half King and his warriors settled, Washington sorted out the situation. The surviving French were huddled behind the Virginians for protection, stunned at what had just occurred. The Mingos confiscated most of the French arms, while the English attended to the prisoners. The combined party marched back to Tanaghrisson's bivouac, where Washington conducted another council. He informed the Half King that Governor Dinwiddie eagerly sought a meeting with Washington's ally in arms and awaited his arrival in Winchester. The proposal surprised him, and he reminded Washington that his first responsibility was to his people, who would surely be in danger from the angered French after what had just occurred. Furthermore, he needed to rally the other Ohio tribes to "take up the hatchet" against the French. He sent messengers carrying French scalps to the Delawares and Shawnees, inviting them to join the cause. Washington may have questioned Tanaghrisson on the severity of the attack on the French, but whatever the question, he assured Washington that the French "intentions were evil" and deemed their claims of diplomatic status as "pure pretense." Furthermore, he insisted that had the Virginians "been such fools as to let them go," the Indians would no longer aid Washington in his efforts against the French. Inexperienced, Washington absorbed the words of the Iroquois elder and later utilized them in explaining his actions to Lieutenant Governor Dinwiddie.[101]

When the council ended, Washington and his men escorted the prisoners to Great Meadows. Once away from the Indians, the French protested Washington's actions, insisting that they had only been sent with a summons to order Washington off the French lands under the protection of "embassy." While clearly they had been sent with the summons from Contrecoeur, the French commander's orders also clearly assigned them to reconnoiter and inform him of what they found before delivering the said summons, and Washington now had those orders in his possession. Still, they fervently insisted that they had come only to order the British away with such veracity that Washington "admired their assurance." They asked Washington if he regarded them "as an Ambassador, or Prisoners of War." He unhesitatingly replied that it was the latter and explained his reasoning.[102]

After returning to Great Meadows, Washington penned an after-action report to Dinwiddie. Remarkably, the first topic of that missive referred to the lieutenant governor's response to the complaints Washington and his officers had previously lodged about their status as officers. Dinwiddie's sharp rebuke of Washington no doubt startled him, and he felt it necessary to address. It may be that Washington received Dinwiddie's letter dated May 25 from Winchester when he returned to the meadows from the Jumonville mission. Regardless, Washington wrote, "I am much concerned that your Honor should seem to charge me with ingratitude for your generous, and my undeserved favors, for I assure you Honorable Sir, nothing is a greater stranger to my Breast, or a Sin that my Soul more abhors than that black and detestable one Ingratitude." He went on to express his appreciation and explain his reasonings on the original complaints before getting to the attack on the French. While many historians have viewed the format of this letter as a form of self-incrimination over his actions at Jumonville, it may simply be that Washington considered his actions and the surrounding circumstances as part of his mission given his orders. But having just successfully completed the first tactical mission of his military career, Washington may have been more unnerved that his prior actions had diminished his standing in the eyes of Robert Dinwiddie, the man who had entrusted Washington with so much responsibility.[103]

To better his odds against likely French retaliation, Washington promptly notified his nominal commander, Colonel Fry at Wills Creek, of the fight at Jumonville. "By some of their papers, we can discover that large detachments are expected every day," wrote Washington, "and we may reasonably suppose are to attack us, especially since we have begun." Given the situation, he urgently requested Fry to rush reinforcements to the front immediately. If reinforcements did not arrive quickly, Washington warned that he "must either quit our ground and return to you or fight very unequal numbers." Unfortunately, Fry had fallen from his horse and faced a lengthy convalescence from a serious injury. Even before Dinwiddie had learned of the Jumonville engagement, he had already directed Fry to turn command over to Major George Muse, who must "proceed with your Officers and Soldiers in your present detachment to join Colo. Washington with all expedition." Muse failed to move, and on June 2, Dinwiddie unloaded on him. "You will not be surprised," wrote the governor, "at my telling you that

I am not well pleased at the tediousness of your march at a time when you should not have lost a moment." He continued, "It is necessary that you should not waste any more time and therefore I send You this Order for You to quit the Wagons, &c., and march immediately to join Col. Washington with the utmost Expedition."[104]

Meanwhile, Washington's confidence grew in the days after the engagement. Although a French counterstrike weighed on his mind, he began to underestimate French resolve in the region. "If the whole detachment of the French behave with no more Resolution than this chosen party did," declared Washington to Dinwiddie on June 3, "I flatter myself we shall have no great trouble in driving them to…Montreal."[105]

Chapter 5

"MY BEST ENDEAVORS SHALL NOT BE WANTING"

The Challenges of Command

On May 29, Washington wrote to Dinwiddie, who had by then arrived at Winchester in hopes of conferencing with the Half King and other Native American leaders. He explained the developments that led to the engagement. He reported that he met with Half King "and got his assent to go hand in hand and strike the French," leaving no doubt that Washington intended to assume the offensive against the French and acknowledged the Native American's role in planning the action. He described the French position as "a very obscure place surrounded by rocks." He noted that "in conjunction with the Half King and Monacatoocha, formed a disposition to attack them on all sides which we accordingly did and after an engagement of about fifteen minutes, we killed ten, wounded one and took twenty-one prisoners." Among the prisoners were two officers who in Washington's words "pretend they were coming on an embassy." Washington failed to reveal how the Half King had killed Jumonville in cold blood after he had been wounded and the French were surrendering. In the aftermath of the engagement, Washington reported that he expected "every hour to be attacked and by unequal numbers, which I must understand if there is 5 to 1 or else, I fear the consequence will be we shall lose the Indians if we suffer ourselves to be drove back." "Let them come what hour they will," wrote the Virginian. With a flourish of youthful bravado born of his recent success, he promised Dinwiddie that "my best endeavors shall not be wanting." Recognizing the odds against him, Washington prophetically added that "[if you hear of my defeat], you will at the same time hear that we have done our duty in fighting as long as there was a possibility of hope."[106]

On May 30, Washington sent Lieutenant John West, Mr. Spindorph (the Swedish gentleman) and twenty men to escort the prisoners to Winchester. Before departing, Washington furnished the two French officers "some necessary clothing by which I have disfurnished myself." At Great Meadows, the Virginians readied for the expected French counterattack. They initiated the construction of a small fort that consisted of logs driven into the ground lengthwise in a circular fashion that measured fifty-three feet in diameter, with a small log cabin in the center to protect supplies and ammunition from the weather and any ill-disciplined Virginians. They constructed breastworks on wet ground outside the palisade in a sort of diamond fashion. When finished, it would be a crude affair, situated in a low meadow with two nearby streams that Washington troops could utilize as breastworks. Washington bragged to Dinwiddie that this "small, palisaded Fort in which with my small numbers I shall not fear the attack of 500 men." Washington referred to the structure as "Fort Necessity" in his journal on June 25.[107]

When Dinwiddie received Washington's report on the action at Jumonville Glen, he considered it "the very agreeable account of your killing and taking Monsieur Le Force and his whole party of 35 men." The governor "heartily" congratulated Washington on his "success." Dinwiddie hoped that Washington's action convinced the Indians "that the French are not invincible when fairly engaged with the English." He cautioned Washington not to let "the good spirits of your soldiers" tempt him "to make any hazardous attempts against too numerous enemy." He encouraged patience and reminded the young man that more vigorous actions could be taken when Fry's detachment of the Virginia Regiment and Captain Mackay's Independent Company of Regulars arrived. Dinwiddie closed the message with "Pray God preserve you in all your proceedings and grant success to our arms," an acknowledgement that a state of war existed in the Ohio Country.[108]

Dinwiddie also hoped that the Half King would journey to Winchester and council with the lieutenant governor. However, the Half King considered the situation too volatile in the Ohio Country and would not leave his people in a time of crisis. In the meantime, Dinwiddie forwarded a large assortment of goods to Washington for distribution to the Indians. To assist with Indian relations, he engaged George Croghan as an interpreter on behalf of "His Majesty" and urged Washington to "shew him proper regard" and consult

FORT NECESSITY — 1754
Rt. 40 — East of Uniontown, Pa.

Postcard of Fort Necessity, circa 1930–45. *Tichnor Brothers Collection, Boston Public Library.*

with him on negotiations with the Indians. Andrew Montour would also be arriving with "a belt and string of wampum," to be used as Washington determined. Dinwiddie also delved into his "private store" of liquor and forwarded some good rum to Washington and his officers.[109]

While Washington waited for the arrival of reinforcements, he worked on improving relations with the Native Americans. Small bands of Indians straggled into the Virginians' camp at Great Meadows. On June 1, nearly "100 persons, including women and children" arrived. Prominent among them were the Half King and Queen Aliquippa, leader of a small band of Senecas who lived near the Youghiogheny and whom Washington had visited during his trip to the French forts in 1753. The aging queen's health prohibited her from actively participating in the councils, so she asked Washington to give her son an English name and permit him to act on her behalf. Washington obtained the approval of the Half King and named him "Colonel Fairfax," which he explained meant "the first of the council." The Half King informed Washington that he had dispatched Monacatoocha to Logstown "with Wampum and four French scalps." He warned the Wyandots and other Iroquois gathered there that "the French had tricked them out of their lands," but fortunately, the English arrived to join hands with the Native Americans and "drive the French beyond the lakes." After delivering the message at Logstown, Monacatoocha set out to

This is an example of wampum, an Indian method of communicating. This belt is a call to arms and war. Tanaghrisson hoped that other tribes would join him after his victory over Jumonville. Located at the Fort Necessity National Battlefield Visitors Center. *Author photo.*

rally the Indians from the Ohio Country to the cause and lead them back to Great Meadows. These developments seemed to bode well for Dinwiddie's desire to build alliances with the Ohio Native Americans.[110]

On Sunday June 2, Washington's day included "prayers in the Fort." A few Shawnee and Delaware families (with few warriors) straggled into the meadows, but the number failed to match the expectation that Tanaghrisson had set. Washington gathered the Natives for the presentation of a ceremonial gift to the Half King from Governor Dinwiddie, a gorget engraved with the likeness of King George II. As a further honor, Washington bestowed the honorary name of Dinwiddie on the Half King, telling him that it meant "the head of everything." Honorifics aside, the reality was that few able-bodied warriors had joined Washington, and the growing number of people strained his logistical ability to feed and care for them. He proposed that the women and children be sent east to live with English settlers, where they could be cared for at a safe distance from the brewing conflict in the Ohio Country. The Half King listened to the proposal but took it under advisement for the time being. Washington looked forward to the arrival of Montour, as the Virginian had no reliable interpreter to assist in his communications and negotiations with the Native Americans. "I am often at a loss how to behave and should be relieved from many anxious fears of offending them if Montour was here," he told Dinwiddie.[111]

Washington soon learned that Fry had died from his injuries at Wills Creek. Dinwiddie promptly promoted Washington to full colonel and the dawdling Muse to lieutenant colonel. Dinwiddie also promised that Colonel James Innes, "an old, experienced officer," would serve as the commander of all English force when he arrived. Innes was expected "daily" at Winchester with his regiment of North Carolina volunteers, but his incompetence thus far exceeded that of Muse. Desertion and disorganization decimated the command, and neither Innes nor his Carolinians participated in the campaign.

While Innes never arrived to assume command, his commission from Dinwiddie and its accompanying orders revealed his continued aggressive intentions against Fort Duquesne. To Innes, Dinwiddie "ordered and directed, as soon as Your united Forces shall be sufficient, to repair thither, and summons the French possessing it to surrender the fort and evacuate the King of G.B. Lands. And in Case of refusal, you are to use Your utmost efforts to compel and force them." The governor went on to describe the disposition of French prisoners after the capture of the force of either sending them to Williamsburg or down the Ohio River to Mississippi.

A fanciful depiction of a council of war at Fort Necessity. *Darlington Collection of Engravings, University of Pittsburgh.*

In short, Dinwiddie maintained his aggressive approach in the Ohio Country, even urging the capture of Fort Duquesne. Washington's actions at Jumonville Glen were only the first step in the larger, aggressive plan fully authorized and directed by Dinwiddie in Williamsburg, not by a spark struck by an impetuous twenty-two-year-old Virginian in the backwoods of Western Pennsylvania.[112]

On June 9, Lieutenant Colonel Muse led the remaining troops of the Virginia Regiment into the camp at Great Meadows. He also brought the welcome news that Captain Mackay's Company had reached Wills Creek and would soon arrive at the meadows. Muse brought with him nine swivel guns, along with appropriate powder and balls. Captain Robert Stobo, a wealthy Scotsman from Williamsburg who was also a friend and relation of Dinwiddie, came with ten servants and a butt of madeira. Stobo proved a capable officer and was soon made regimental engineer. Captain Andrew Montour also arrived with a commission to command a planned company of Indian scouts. Reports of French activity in the region filtered into Washington's camp. On June 10, reports arrived stating that "some French were advancing towards us." Washington promptly dispatched a party of Native Americans toward Gist's Plantation. While they were out, a false alarm rattled the Virginians at midnight. Two Indians reported back the next morning, telling of "a small party of French," while the rest of the band continued the scout to Stuart's Crossing on the Youghiogheny, modern Connellsville, Pennsylvania.[113]

Feeling emboldened with Muse's arrival, Washington ordered out the Virginia Regiment in the hopes of finding a large party of French deserters that recent French deserters claimed were out there. It may have been a ruse on the part of the French, but Washington went all in believing that a large party of Frenchmen was ready to switch sides. He ordered Muse to guard the fort and supplies while he marched with 130 men and 30 Indians under Montour. It wasn't long before word came back that there were only 9 French deserters, although they insisted that 100 more French troops "were only waiting for a favorable opportunity to come and join us." More importantly, they informed Washington that Captain Contrecoeur was awaiting the arrival of 400 men at Fort Duquesne. Furthermore, they had nearly completed the fort with strong artillery. To make the news even worse, Washington learned that the Delaware and Shawnee tribes "had taken up the hatchet" against the English. In an attempt to sway them to his cause, he invited them to a council that would take place at Gist's settlement.[114]

On June 10, Washington complained to Dinwiddie that there were not enough provisions on hand at the fort to feed the regiment for two days. He and his Virginians felt "extremely ill-used" by the failure of Major Carlyle's deputies to deliver supplies as promised. The situation pained Washington, as he knew that Carlyle, whom he considered a gentleman, took "pains to ensure satisfaction." Instead, the middlemen received funds but failed to deliver the promised goods. Carlyle apologized for the failure but only confirmed Washington's suspicions about the suppliers. He noted that Pennsylvanian George Croghan had contracted to deliver "10,000 Wt. of flour" by June 15, but time soon revealed to Carlyle that Croghan did not have four hundred pounds on hand. On June 17, Carlyle reported that he had contracted with Christopher Gist to deliver flour in thirty days and that there were "50,000 wt" then at the mills and that when the "new crops come in, you shall have plenty." Promised provisions meant little at the front, as the Virginia Regiment needed flour now, and the lack of food weakened the troops when they needed most to be ready for action.[115]

On June 14, Captain James Mackay arrived with his Independent Company of one hundred Regulars from South Carolina. A herd of sixty cattle accompanied them, also bringing a five-day supply of much-needed flour. Mackay's arrival also confused the command situation. Although Washington was a colonel in command of the Virginia Regiment, Captain James Mackay, the commander of the Regular company, held a king's commission in the Regular British army. Washington's commission came from the colonial Lieutenant Governor Dinwiddie. This placed Washington in a subservient position to Captain Mackay. Prior to their arrival, Dinwiddie told Washington that Mackay "appears to be an officer of some experience and importance, you will with Colo. Fry and Colo. Innes so well agree as not to let some Punctilio's about command render the service you are all engaged in [to be] perplexed or obstructed."[116]

Washington assured Dinwiddie that he would make every effort to respect Mackay and his rank and urge his officers to do the same. Washington worried that his men who had thus far borne the suffering of the campaign would take offense at the presence of the more highly paid Regulars. "We have the same spirit to serve our Gracious King as they have; and are as ready and willing to sacrifice our lives for our Country's good as them," he proclaimed to Dinwiddie, "and here once more and for the last time I must say this will be a canker that will grate some officers of this Regiment." Although not appreciated by Dinwiddie, Washington's point was well made and truthful, and he owed it to his command to make it. From a more practical point of view, Washington requested Dinwiddie to send direct orders delineating who would be in command of the expedition. "I would be particularly obliged if your Honor had declared whether he was under my Command or Independent of it." The young Virginian cautiously added that "I shall be studious to avoid all disputes that may tend to public prejudice, but as far as I am able will inculcate harmony and unanimity."[117]

Dinwiddie did not address Washington's request. Instead, he believed that his appointment of Colonel James Innes as commander and chief of the expedition would resolve the situation. As noted earlier, Innes and his command failed to arrive in time to engage the French in the coming action and as such provided no relief to the command situation. Hence, Washington was left dangling to Mackay's peculiarities. It did not take long for problems to arise. Mackay encamped his troops away from the Virginians and maintained his own regime. Washington thought it prudent to share the password and countersign and "place to repair to in case of alarm" with Mackay and his command to ensure security and safety of the overall command. While Mackay recognized the importance, he refused to accept direction from Washington.

"Then who is to give it," lamented Washington to Dinwiddie. "How absurd is obvious." Furthermore, the Regulars refused to assist in the critical task of road building. Regulars were due extra pay for such work, and Washington had no funds to provide. Furthermore, why would he when his men had been building roads through the mountains all the way from Wills Creek? To pay the Regulars extra for fatigue duty would only demoralize the Virginians. "I therefore shall continue to complete the work we have began with my poor fellows." He also proudly emphasized, "The first column of the Virginia Regiment has done more for the interest of this expedition than any company or corps that will hereafter arrive."[118]

On a personal level, Colonel Washington found Captain Mackay to be "a very good sort of gentleman." The Virginian assured the Scotsman "in the most serious manner" that he would take pleasure "in consulting and advising with him upon all occasions." While Washington was willing to work with Mackay, he refused to subordinate command of the Virginia Regiment to the Scotsman. Although the Virginians served at lower pay than the Regulars, they still had their pride, and as George told the governor, "We always hoped to enjoy the rank of officers which to me Sir is much dearer than the pay."[119]

Regardless of the difficulties, Washington remained focused on his mission, the primary goal of which was the capture of Fort Duquesne. The

English viewed this as the recapture of His Majesty's fort that had fallen to the French in April. To do so would require the reinforcements from the two New York Independent Companies and Innes's North Carolinians, all which Dinwiddie had assured him were en route. Although he lacked the resources to accomplish this on his own now, Washington could prepare. Furthermore, the British hopes for a strategic alliance with substantial Native American groups rested almost exclusively at this point with Monacatoocha and his diplomatic journey to sway the Ohio tribes to the English side. Washington learned that he planned to return up the Monongahela to Redstone Creek, so the Virginian determined to move in that direction. The Monongahela also offered a waterborne route to Fort Duquesne, so Redstone again became Washington's objective. To get there, Washington needed to build and improve the road from Great Meadows to Redstone that could accommodate the supply wagons and heavy artillery that pending reinforcements would haul from Alexandria.

Washington departed Great Meadows on June 16, leaving Mackay's Regulars to hold Fort Necessity. Difficulties emerged almost immediately, with the Virginia Regiment's wagons "breaking very often" on the trek over Chestnut Ridge. They traveled a few miles to Gist's Plantation and halted. He sent a detachment under Captain Andrew Lewis to construct a road to the storehouse at Redstone on the Monongahela. Another detachment under Captain William Polson went in search of food farther up the Monongahela. Problems of another sort soon emerged. The Half King and the other Indians at Fort Necessity disagreed with Washington's decision to move toward Redstone and refused to march with him, remaining at the meadows. Eight Mingos or Ohio Country Iroquois arrived at Gist's on June 18 for the proposed council that Washington had invited the Ohio tribes to, demanding a council with Washington. He stalled them and summoned the Half King. The French had told these Mingos that the English intended to "destroy entirely all your brethren the Indians who will not join you on the road." Washington assured them this was not the case and deferred any council until Tanaghrisson arrived. Delegates from the Delawares and Shawnees also arrived. Upon Tanaghrisson's arrival, Washington began a council that lasted for several days, with speeches by all parties. In the end, Washington failed to sway the Ohio Country Indians to his banner. While some, such as Chief Shingas of the Delawares, harbored private inclinations toward the English, he dared not publicly align with Washington given the known strength of the French and preponderance of the Native Americans siding with them. In

Washington's men hauled their swivel guns and supplies over this range, Chestnut Ridge, on the march to Gist's and the return to Fort Necessity. *Author photo.*

the end, even the Half King abandoned Washington, perhaps miffed that Washington had dealt directly with the Delaware and Shawnee people, who were at least nominally under Tanaghrisson's control.[120]

On June 27, Washington detached a party of three officers and sixty-five men under Captain Andrew Lewis to clear a road to the mouth of Redstone Creek at the Monongahela. He also sent Captain William Polson out on "detachment" to build canoes and go upstream to secure corn from Dunkard settlements in Virginia on the Monongahela River to feed the troops. Washington's situation at Gist's settlement was growing more precarious by the day. On June 28, Monacatoocha arrived at Gist's Plantation with news of the French. He had just returned from Fort Duquesne, where he personally witnessed the arrival of French reinforcements. He estimated that there were eight hundred French soldiers and four hundred Indians. Washington sent orders for the detachments to return and rushed a messenger informing Captain Mackay of the situation and requesting him to bring his Independent Company to Gist's settlement. The doughty Regular officer promptly marched his one hundred Redcoats and arrived at Washington's camp at night. In the meantime, Washington ordered the men to fortify their position at Gist's. Lewis's and Polson's detachments arrived there the next morning. The Virginians gathered all the rails from Gist's settlement "and made a hog pen fort surrounded with standing trees and commanding ground."[121]

With the situation deteriorating by the hour, Washington called his officers together for a council of war. Monacatoocha's information on the reinforcements verified what Washington had learned from the French deserters. Furthermore, he had heard the French "declare their resolution to march and attack the English with 800 of their own men & 400 Indians." Washington and his officers also concluded that two deserters from their force had probably informed the French of "our starving condition and our numbers and situation." The supply of meat and bread had been exhausted for six days, and their remaining twenty-five cattle were primarily milk cows. They had only one quart of salt to preserve meat. In short, Washington's four hundred men would soon be in a starving condition. Remaining at Gist's also allowed the French to take another road that ran directly from Fort Necessity to Redstone, allowing the French to reach the fort and cut off Washington's force at its present location. This would sever his link to reinforcements, supplies and his line of retreat to Wills Creek. They also realized that they could not successfully fight the French in the open ground, as they greatly outnumbered them and knew their situation. Even if they managed to defeat the French and escaped, the English would be "cut to pieces" by the French-allied Indians as they attempted to retreat. Faced with these obstacles, the officers unanimously decided that "it was absolutely necessary to return to our fort at the meadows and wait there until supplied with a stock of provisions to serve us for some months." Ironically, Washington's refusal to remain at the fort, as Tanaghrisson initially suggested, had cost him his few Indian allies at the moment they were most needed, and now he returned having accomplished nothing.[122]

Washington had only "two very indifferent teams, and few horses," so the officers loaded their personal mounts with ammunition. He set the example, ordering his own horse loaded first and paying several soldiers four pistoles, a currency, for carrying his personal belongings. The nine swivel guns were hauled back by men of the Virginia Regiment over "twelve miles of the roughest and most hilly road of any on the Allegheny Mountains." Due to the lack of teams, they had to leave some ammunition behind, burying it in the woods. Mackay's Independents refused to assist with hauling the guns and ammunition, "which had an unhappy effect on our men, who no sooner learned that it was not the proper Duty of Soldiers to perform those services." Captain Stephen observed that "they became as backward as

Archaeologists recovered this log from the entrenchments outside the stockade that were used in the construction of the earthworks. *Author photo.*

the Independents." The march proved harrowing on Washington's already haggard Virginians, and they arrived back at the meadows "very much fatigued." Rations began running out eight days earlier, and it was believed that the foodstuffs promised by Croghan and Carlyle would be waiting for them, but they found only a few bags of flour.[123]

Apparently, there was discussion of continuing the retreat to Wills Creek. However, the physical exertion of building fortifications at Gist's and the strenuous march back to Fort Necessity left the already hungry men too weak to march and haul the swivel guns and ammunition any farther. To abandon those items would be a breach of honor, something that Washington and his officers could not abide. Washington also had intelligence that the New York Independent Companies and supply convoys were at Will's Creek and on their way to join Washington. So, it was "thought most advisable to fortify ourselves in the best manner possible" and await their arrival, "which we daily expected." A messenger dashed toward Will's Creek to inform them of the anticipated French attack on Washington at Great Meadows and to urge the reinforcements onward. Meanwhile, the Virginians "set about clearing the woods nearest us and carrying the logs to raise a breastwork and enlarge the fort."[124]

As the French marched toward their fateful encounter with Colonel George Washington at Great Meadows, his unlucky Virginians suffered a further blow to their cause. Tanaghrisson had urged Washington to remain at the fort. Although the Virginians had returned to the Indians at Great Meadows, reports came in from other Indians telling them of the strength of the approaching French. The Half King assessed the situation and concluded that "the Col. was a good-natured man but had no experience." He treated the Indians like slaves, "had them out scouting every day, and would never take advice from them." Even worse, he failed to build an adequate fort except "that little thing upon the Meadow." Tanaghrisson attempted to guide Washington in the strategy for the coming engagement, but he rebuffed the Native American's ideas, so the Half King and his thirty warriors abandoned Washington when he most needed them. They claimed that he "would never listen to them." Regardless, they were gone, and the French were on the way. There was nothing more that Washington could do now other than to wait and pray that the reinforcements in the form of the New York Independent Companies of Regulars and Innes's North Carolina Regiment that Dinwiddie had promised arrived at Great Meadows before the French did.[125]

Chapter 6

"MY HEART ACHES, AND I SEND THE FRENCH TOMORROW TO AVENGE"

French Retaliation

Early on the morning of May 28, Private Monceau of Jumonville's detachment had just arisen from a rainy night sleeping in a crude cabin nestled in a wooded hollow. As he readied for the day, Washington attacked the French camp. Monceau fled barefooted into the underbrush at the northern end of the bivouac. He briefly watched as Jumonville attempted to have the summons read to Washington but noticed that his comrades were drawn up in platoons situated between the Virginians and the gathering Indians. Monceau did not wait around to see what happened next; he fled across the countryside to Redstone, where he secured a canoe and paddled down the Monongahela to Fort Duquesne. There he delivered the first news of the stunning attack to Captain Contrecoeur, the commander.

The French commander promptly penned a missive to the governor of New France, the Marquis du Quesne, and informed him of the details as he had learned them. Some Mingos who may have been present with the Half King during Washington's attack on Jumonville informed Contrecoeur that the English had killed Jumonville by a musket shot to the head while the summons was being read. They further embellished their tale, claiming that they had rushed between the surviving French and the English to prevent the latter from slaughtering the former. The Indians also reported that Washington's party numbered six hundred men and was an advance to clear a road for a larger force that numbered in the thousands with artillery. Contrecoeur concluded with certainty that the "English are on their March" and requested three hundred men as reinforcements and provisions. He concluded, "If the discovery which has cost our people so dear had not been made, the English would have come upon us unawares; but now we shall be vigilant on all accounts."[126]

Contrecoeur determined to exact vengeance against Washington but decided to await the arrival of reinforcements. By June 26, he had assembled five hundred French soldiers and eleven Indians from the Ohio Country tribes under the command of Captain LeMercier. At 8:00 a.m., Captain Louis Coulon de Villiers, the older brother of the slain Jumonville, arrived at Fort Duquesne in command of a large contingent of at least one hundred Indians from the Great Lakes and Canada.[127]

Captain de Villiers held seniority over LeMercier, and Contrecoeur placed the older, more experienced officer in command of the punitive expedition against Washington. Born in 1710, De Villiers had fought alongside his father, and a musket ball shattered his left arm as they participated in a counterattack after his father had been killed. Although disabled and certified for a pension and continued pay "to provide for his needs," he stayed in active service. With his brother Joseph, he participated in the Chickasaw War in Louisiana and commanded Fort St. Joseph (now Niles, Michigan) from 1743 to 1745. During King George's War, he recruited and organized Indians from the Upper Great Lakes to raid New York. After promotion to lieutenant, he participated in Celeron's expedition to mark the extent of French claims in the Ohio Country. In 1750, he was appointed to command Fort Miami (Fort Wayne, Indiana) until 1753, when he was promoted to captain. Captain de Villiers was an accomplished and respected officer and well prepared for the task at hand.[128]

The Indians who accompanied de Villiers to Fort Duquesne had done so with the understanding that Governor Duquesne had sent them "only to work for good affairs." De Villiers gathered them for a council, during which Contrecoeur explained the changed circumstances in the region as a result of Washington's actions. Contrecoeur urged them to "unclog" their ears so that "my words will fall to your heart, and you feel the same pain that I feel." He told them of the assassination of Jumonville while on a diplomatic mission. "My children," he pleaded with them, "my heart aches, and I send the French tomorrow to avenge." He invited these Indians by a belt of wampum to each tribe "to come and accept the hatchet to accompany your Father and help him crush the English who have violated the strongest laws by assassinating the bearers of words." For good measure, he gifted them "two barrels of wine to make you a feast."[129]

This bronze relief of Fort Duquesne is located at Point State in downtown Pittsburgh on the actual grounds of the fort. Its original footprint is marked today within the park. After the British occupied this area, they constructed Fort Pitt. *Author photo.*

An Iroquois chief protested, arguing that they had come "only to work for good affairs as they did not wish to disturb the earth." The warriors, however, carried off the hatchet and the wine. They returned two hours later, and all accepted the hatchet and sang a song of war. The Indians spent the next day making shoes and other preparations for the expedition to Great Meadows.[130]

While the Indians prepared, Contrecoeur gathered Captains de Villiers, LeMercier and Longueuil to his headquarters. They went over the plan for the expedition and established parameters for the actions to be taken. On June 28, Contrecoeur ordered de Villiers "to depart immediately with the detachment of French and Indians…to meet the English Army," as they showed no regard for the official peace between the two kings. Contrecoeur ordered de Villiers "to attack them if he sees a day to do so and destroy them if he can to chastise them for the assassination of our messenger, which they did to us by violating the rights of civilized nations." Despite the desire for vengeance, Contrecoeur cautioned de Villiers to "avoid all cruelty as much as he can."[131]

By ten o'clock on the morning of June 28, de Villiers had distributed provisions to the troops and set out with five hundred French Marines and Canadian militia and more than one hundred Native Americans to avenge the death of his younger brother, Jumonville. They headed up the Monongahela River in their canoes with Indian scouts, while French cadets scoured the shore to avoid any surprises. They canoed to a point about five hundred yards before the junction with the Youghiogheny River, where they camped for the night. There, de Villiers conferred with a chief from an Ohio River tribe regarding the route, and he suggested avoiding the Youghiogheny River, as the water was too low. On the morning of June 30, the Catholic French celebrated Mass in camp. Then they continued upstream until they reached the Ohio Company's storehouse on Redstone Creek.

There the French disembarked, and de Villiers examined the storehouse, noting that it was "made of stacked logs, well crenelated [viz. outfitted with

British weapons and accoutrements and musket balls fired at Great Meadows, on display at Fort Necessity National Battlefield. *Author photo.*

loopholes for firing muskets], and about thirty feet long by twenty-two feet wide." The French commander conferred with his Indian allies frequently, as he wanted to keep them in good stead. The force encamped for the night near the storehouse, and de Villiers and his officers conferred again with the chief. They discussed "precautions to be taken for the safety of our pirogues, and the people who were to guard them." They agreed that twenty men would be left at the storehouse to guard the canoes, as they could make a strong resistance from the fortified building.[132]

On July 1, de Villiers left twenty men and some sick Indians under "a good sergeant" to guard the canoes and unnecessary equipment at the storehouse. Scouts were sent out in advance to guard against surprise. Ammunition was issued to the men, and then they marched in the direction of the highlands to the east. The road was rough, and the Catholic priest soon wore out under the strain, so he gave the army a general absolution and returned to Redstone. They soon encountered tracks nearby and concluded that they had been discovered. Not receiving any reports from the scouts, de Villiers dispatched another party with the same mission. They soon encountered the first scouting detachment and narrowly avoided a friendly-fire incident. Concluding that the English certainly knew the French were en route in force, de Villiers continued the advance to a "dwelling." The captain

French weapons and accoutrements at Fort Necessity National Battlefield. *Author photo.*

noted that it was "situated advantageously from discovery on all sides" and posted his troops to defend themselves in case of an attack. They spent the night there waiting back for further reports from the scouts.[133]

The march continued the next morning without any information from the lookouts. As they moved across the countryside, the Indians who had stayed at Redstone caught up to the column, having captured an English deserter along the way. De Villiers questioned him, threatening to hang him "if he imposed on me." He revealed that Washington had abandoned his post at Gist's place and returned to Fort Necessity with his swivel guns. They marched to Gist's, which Washington had abandoned a few days earlier. De Villiers noted that the settlement "consisted of three houses surrounded by posts and fence, the protection of which was commanded by the neighboring heights." The French searched the house and confiscated "several caches of tools and ancillaries." With rain pouring from the sky, they spent the night there.[134]

Captain de Villiers knew that he was close to the English fort. He had also learned that the English were short of food and had about four hundred men on hand. He interrogated the deserter again and conferred with the Indians. He determined that they would attack in the morning and promised his Native American allies that he would not expose them recklessly in the coming action. The rains continued to pour the next morning, but the French force moved forward with a party of Indians serving as advance scouts. De Villiers concluded that the rain would work to their advantage and hopefully permit the English to let their guard down. As the column moved out, the Nipissing and Algonquin Indians refused to participate, so he continued with the other "nations," which shamed the recalcitrant allies to rejoin the mission. De Villiers's opportunity for vengeance would soon be at hand.

Chapter 7

"A LAMENTABLE AFFAIR"

The Battle of Fort Necessity

At daybreak on July 3, Captain de Villiers deployed Indian scouts to learn the precise disposition of Washington's force at Great Meadows. Scouts soon captured and brought back three prisoners who "came from the Shawnee," likely Native Americans abandoning Washington's cause. After obtaining information from them, the French halted briefly at the glen where de Villiers's lamented brother Ensign Jumonville and his party had been attacked. Scalped and unburied corpses lay scattered over the ground, and a severed head had been impaled on a branch implanted in the wet ground. The French properly buried the dead, and general prayers were offered on behalf of their souls. It was surely a solemn moment for the French commander and steeled his resolve in fulfilling his mission as his command closed in on Washington. De Villiers then addressed his Indian allies on the ground where his brother had been killed and explained "the vengeance he hoped to have with their help." His stirring speech struck a chord with his Native American allies, and they pledged their assistance in the vendetta before the six-hundred-man force moved toward Great Meadows.[135]

At dawn, as rain began to fall from the cloudy sky, one of the advanced French scouts shot an outlying English sentry in the leg, providing Washington his first concrete evidence that the French were lurking nearby. Washington had roughly three hundred effective troops from his own and Mackay's commands available for battle, with about one hundred others sick or otherwise incapacitated. Washington set them quickly to work expanding and improving the entrenchments "in the greatest confusion," but it was

Robert Griffing's *A Charming Field for an Encounter*, portraying Washington forming up his troops to confront the French at Great Meadows.

too little too late. The fortifications should have been improved in the weeks after the engagement at Jumonville when Washington could have done so in a more planned and deliberate manner. Private John Shaw described the trenches as being "about two foot deep." Major Adam Stephen oversaw the cutting of more logs to strengthen the stockade and had several of the swivel guns mounted on logs driven into the soft, muddy ground. At one point, he tore down part of the stockade to improve the field of fire for the swivel guns. More information would soon arrive on the extent of the French force. Although Washington's Native American allies had refused to stand and fight with him at Great Meadows, two Indians spotted the French that morning and ran back to the fort. They arrived at 9:00 a.m. and warned Washington that the enemy "were within four miles of us, that they were a very numerous body."[136]

When the French arrived within two and a half miles from the fort, de Villiers dispatched more scouts toward Great Meadows. Behind them, he

deployed his troops into three columns, "with each officer in his division to be able to dispose of it according to the necessity." The French advanced over the remaining ground in "orderly fashion" until a little before 11:00 a.m., when an English sentinel saw them and fired a warning shot that brought all work to a halt at the fort. Washington and Mackay ordered their men into line, and soldiers grabbed their muskets and scurried into the battle line. Washington deployed them into line of battle in the open ground immediately southeast of the fort. Washington and Mackay determined to advance into the meadow and engage the French in the open. Meanwhile, French scouts reported to de Villiers that they had been discovered and that the English were "in battle array to attack us." De Villiers decided that he would fight in "battle formation suitable for woodland combat." He posted his men in a loosely arrayed formation and approached the fort from the western edge of the meadow on an old Indian trail that Washington had improved into a military road.

They deployed into firing formation and delivered an ineffective long-range volley toward the English at six hundred yards, the lead balls falling harmlessly to the ground well short of Washington's position. If they hoped

Above: View of Fort Necessity from the perspective of the French on the higher ground from a point located about 150 yards southwest of the fort. *Author photo.*

Opposite: Battle of Fort Necessity, based on J.C. Harrington's map in *New Light on Washington's Fort Necessity* and maps on interpretive markers at Fort Necessity National Battlefield. *Map by George Chakvetadze.*

to intimidate the British, the tactic did not work. Then the French followed that path into the woods on the meadow's southern fringe, aiming for a point of woods nearer Washington's troops. As the French advanced, they presented their left flank toward the fort, and Washington's men opened fire from the two swivel guns that Major Stephen had deployed on the breastworks just outside the palisade.[137]

Colonel Washington rode tall in his saddle and cut a commanding figure as he deployed his troops into two lines of battle. With combat moments away, the friction between Washington and Mackay seemingly vanished, and the Virginian rode forward with Mackay's South Carolina Independents, leading the advance to take possession of a point of woods before the French reached it. The lightly regarded Lieutenant Colonel George Muse led the Virginia Regiment, but the skittish Muse spied the French and Indians coming down a hill toward the point of woods and panicked. He turned to the Virginians and called out that the French were

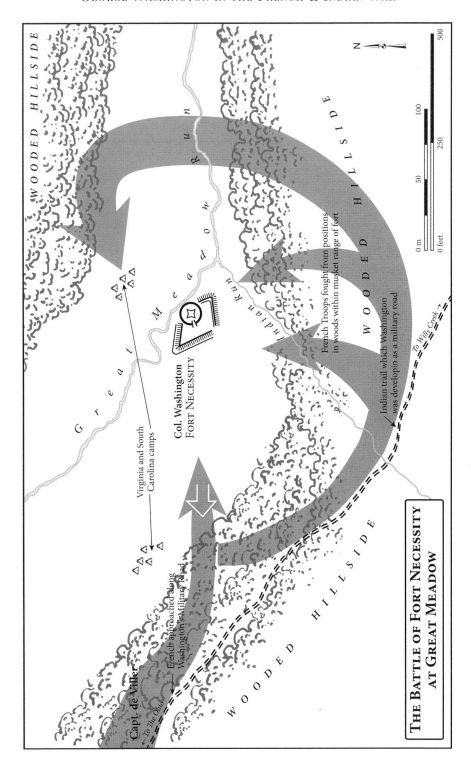

WOODED HILLSIDE

N

500

100

250

50

0 m

0 feet

Indian Run

Great Meadow

Run

French Troops fought from positions
in woods within musket range of fort

WOODED HILLSIDE

To Wills Creek →

Col. Washington
FORT NECESSITY

Indian trail which Washington
was developin as a military road

Virginia and South
Carolina camps

WOODED HILLSIDE

Capt. de Villier

French approached along
Washington's Military Road

To The Ohio →

WOODED HILLSIDE

**THE BATTLE OF FORT NECESSITY
AT GREAT MEADOW**

going to capture the fort. Instead of attacking with the South Carolinians, Muse "frightened them [his Virginians] back to the same trenches where they were galled on all sides by 1,100 French and Indians who never came into the open ground." Muse personally "ran back in the utmost confusion, happy he that could get into the Fort first." He was later censured for his cowardice and omitted from the list of officers formally thanked by the House of Burgesses. With the Virginians withdrawing, the French and Indians focused their musket fire on Washington and the South Carolina Independents. Washington and Mackay's Regulars trudged back through the muddy meadow to the entrenchments, where they took shelter and prepared to meet their attackers.[138]

De Villiers had hoped to strike the British in the open. His French Marines, militia and Indians "let out a yell" and advanced, but before they could drive home the attack, the Regulars retreated "to their entrenchments, which held their strength." De Villiers assessed the terrain and relative positions that both sides occupied. He quickly saw that the fort sat in the low center of the boggy meadow and that the woods surrounding it provided concealment and cover for his French and Indian troops while still being within musket range. With this advantage, de Villiers "endeavored to invest the fort." He advanced his men as closely as possible, carefully avoiding the unnecessary exposure of "the subjects of his Majesty in vain" against the entrenched British. After Washington withdrew to the entrenchments, he initially held his fire, anticipating that the French and Indians would continue their advance and rush the fort. At one point, the French encouraged "their Indians to advance out of the wood, and show themselves," near the entrenchments, but Washington saw the developing movement and directed his troops' musketry at it, stopping the threat at its inception. When it became apparent that they would not rashly charge across the meadow, he ordered the troops to open fire on the concealed adversaries. The French Marines and Indians unleashed an accurate storm of lead that soon forced the English to abandon their swivel guns and ringed the fort with "a galling fire." The sulfuric smoke hung in the humid air over the meadow, as both sides maintained a heavy rate of fire. Captain de Villiers worried that "the fervor and zeal of our Canadians and soldiers" would consume their ammunition supply if they maintained the rapid rate of fire. The French had only the ammunition that each man carried, and it was early in the engagement. The French commander examined a position "that seemed to me the most suited to wiping them out with a sortie." Looking across the open ground, de Villiers declined to make a sudden thrust but instead maneuvered troops

French soldiers attacking Fort Necessity, from a diorama at the Fort Necessity National Battlefield. *Author photo.*

around to the east and north to seal off Washington's line of retreat while he prepared defenses for the coming night. In moving toward this rising ground, the French and Indians confiscated "caches of food, ammunition, and merchandise," booty that heightened morale among the Canadian militiamen and Indians.[139]

While the French fired their muskets from the relative security of the woods and maneuvered, Washington's soldiers endured life in the rain-filled trenches with French bullets whizzing among them from all directions. The sickening *thud* of lead missiles striking flesh and bone was heard all too often. This was Colonel Washington's first real lesson in war, and the charm of the whistling bullets at Jumonville Glen had certainly worn off. Despite the heavy French and Indian musketry, Washington moved about his men without regard for the danger, leading a seemingly charmed life as one-third of the men around him fell dead or wounded. The heavy precipitation that had fallen throughout the day "set everything afloat in the Encampment, which was in a natural meadow or dry marsh." The trenches were "half full of water, and [the] fort half [a] leg deep of mud." As casualties mounted, blood mixed with the water, turning the trenches into troughs filled with a macabre stew of gore. Regardless, Major Stephen worked feverishly to keep the men supplied with ammunition, his hands and face blackened by the powder. The extreme soggy conditions caused most muskets to misfire and clog due to wet powder, but the Virginia Regiment had only a few tools to remove the soggy loads and return the weapons to proper firing condition. As they struggled in the mire, the aimed fire of the experienced French soldiers and their Indian allies inflicted a heavy toll on Washington's force. Private John Shaw recalled that men inside the stockade were wounded when French musket balls struck the shed and sent splinters flying into them. By the time dusk settled on Great Meadows, nearly one hundred of Washington's men had been killed or wounded. Hemmed in by the French and their allies, with vivid tales of Indians scalping their captives circulating among the men, half of Washington's Virginians broke into the rum stores and became intoxicated. This serious breach of military order contrasted starkly with Washington and Mackay's official portrayal of the men behaving with "singular intrepidity…determined to sell our Lives as dearly as possibly we could."[140]

The situation was probably slightly better among Mackay's Independent Regulars, who were more disciplined and presumably better equipped than the Virginians. They, too, suffered under the accurate French musketry, losing thirty out of one hundred soldiers killed or wounded in the engagement. Lieutenant Peter Mercier, "a Gentleman of true military Worth," bravely led his men in the combat and fought on even after he was wounded until a second musket ball plunged into his body. As devoted soldiers carried him to the surgeon inside the stockade, a third bullet snuffed out his life.[141] On top of the human toll, Washington reported, "The enemy had deprived us of all our creatures; by killing in the beginning of the engagement, our horses, cattle, and every living thing they could, even to the very dogs."[142]

The fighting waned, Washington later reported, when the "most tremendous rain that can be conceived" fell from the sky, temporarily halting the combat. The situation looked hopeless for Washington and his command, as the French had virtually encircled their position, and the British could see no way out. Washington scanned his position and saw that he had lost nearly one-third of his effective force either killed or wounded—thirty killed and seventy wounded. Blood, mud and water were everywhere. The French commander noted that the fire of Washington's troops "was rekindled at six o'clock in the evening with more vigor than ever and lasted until eight o'clock."[143]

Washington's defensive position at Fort Necessity, as shown in a diorama at the Fort Necessity National Battlefield Visitor Center. *Author photo.*

From the same diorama, this section shows French-allied Native Americans fighting from the cover of the woods opposite Fort Necessity. *Author photo.*

Remarkably, the situation with the French was not as optimistic as Washington and his men likely believed it to be. De Villiers had lost only three killed and seventeen wounded fighting behind "every little rising-tree-stump-stone-and bush" while maintaining an accurate musketry into the British. Nevertheless, de Villiers reported, "As we had been soaked by the rain all day, the detachment was very tired, and the Indians announced their intent to depart the next day." De Villiers also received reports of "drums beating in the distance and cannon fire," supposedly approaching British reinforcements from Wills Creek. He conferred with the French second in command, Captain LeMercier, and the two men agreed to offer the British a ceasefire and parley.[144]

As darkness came over the damp, depressing scene at Great Meadows, the French called out, "Voulez vous parler [Do you want to talk]?" Washington initially suspected a French ruse and declined the offer. After all, the French force outnumbered the English and occupied commanding ground around the fort. After some delay, the French again called out, offering to parley. This time, Washington sent Captain Jacob Van Braam, his French interpreter from his 1753 excursion to Fort Le Boeuf, and Lieutenant Peronie, a French Huguenot who had settled in Virginia, across the lines to hear the French proposals. Given the direness of the situation among Washington's command, the French offer of parley came as a surprise to the men, who thought they were on the verge of being overrun and exposed to the barbarities of de Villiers's Indian allies. LeMercier received Van Braam in the French lines and escorted the Dutchman to de Villiers. The French commander recounted the conversation:[145]

> [N]ot being at war, we wished to avoid the cruelties on the part of the Indians to which they would expose themselves if they obstinately persisted in their resistance. That night we would deprive them of all hope of escape, that we now consented to give them pardon, having come only to avenge the assassination of my brother made by violating the most sacred Laws, and compelling them to free themselves from the lands of the King's dominion, and we agreed with them to grant them capitulations.[146]

Washington reported that Van Braam returned with the French proposals, which were agreed to "about Midnight." He reviewed the rain-spattered agreement with Washington and Mackay in the dead of night by candlelight. The capitulation document contained two references to the "assassination" of Jumonville, but at the time, Washington made no mention of it. Given that the word *assassination* is quite similar in French and English, it was not a word that needed much interpretation. At the time, Washington objected to giving up his "munitions de guerre" and had it struck from the agreement, to which de Villiers agreed. In the official report attributed jointly to Washington and Mackay and widely published, the essence of the French terms was that "we agreed that each side should retire without molestation, they back to their Fort at Monongahela, and we to Wills Creek: That we should march away with all the Honors of War, and with all our stores, effects and baggage." While that description is superficially factually, it leaves the impression of a balanced agreement. The rest of the report likewise completely downplayed the scope of the defeat and greatly exaggerated French casualties as well as the terms of the capitulation. However, the actual terms of the agreement contained much more detailed language, including a damning admission of the assassination signed by Washington and Mackay.

De Villiers acknowledged that peace existed between the two kings and that his only objective had been to "revenge the Assassination committed on one of our Officers." As such, he permitted Washington to retire with his force and belongings, except his artillery, "to his own country" and to restrain, "as much as it shall be in our power, the Indians that are with us." De Villiers further allowed Washington to depart with "the Honors of War, that they march out with drums beating and one Swiviel gun to convince them we treat them as friends." He allowed them to "hide their effects and to come again, and search for them, when they have a Number of Horses sufficient to carry them off," provided that the English "give their Word of Honor, to work no more upon any Buildings in this Place, or any Part on this Side the Mountains." The agreement also required Washington to leave behind two hostages, Captains Van Braam and Stobo, to guarantee the return of the French prisoners taken at Jumonville Glen.[147]

At sunrise on the Fourth of July 1754, the rains ceased, and Washington prepared for his retreat. Inside the little fort, men broke open the barrels of black powder and scattered it over the muddy ground and puddles, rendering it useless. Washington realized that he had dress clothing that he would not be able to carry with him. Never one to lose an opportunity to recoup a financial loss, he sold it to Van Braam, one of the hostages, for pay due him. Washington also called for volunteers to carry officers' personal belongings. He assured the soldiers that "whatever they carried would be their own" if they were not paid for their efforts. One of Captain Mackay's Regulars volunteered to carry Washington's rifle. When Washington sought its return later that summer, Mackay reminded Washington of his promise

Listing of known dead from the Battle of Fort Necessity at the visitor center. *Author photo.*

and informed him that the soldier desired another rifle in return; he assured George that the rifle would be forthcoming. What they could not carry was destroyed so that nothing would be left behind, or so Washington thought. Some of his personal belongings were abandoned, including his journal, which fell into French hands and became a source of controversy for him.[148]

Meanwhile, de Villiers led the French troops with drums beating and Indians to the fort and deployed them in two ranks. Washington and Mackay formed their tired, wet and in some cases hungover soldiers into columns and marched out of the fort with flags flying and drums beating, filing between the two ranks of their French and Indian adversaries. As the British passed, they noticed among the Indians some who had previously professed allegiance to Washington and spent time in their camp at Great Meadows. While the agreement permitted them to take one swivel gun with them, they lacked horses and manpower to carry it and left it behind. De Villiers assessed the scene as Washington led the lucky survivors away from Great Meadows. The sight of so many dead and wounded moved the French commander "to pity them despite the resentment which I had for the manner" that they had killed his brother. Then the French occupied the fort. Upon entering it, one Frenchman recalled that it was in "a state of absolute havoc."[149]

Several incidents occurred as Washington prepared to leave the fort and after they had departed Great Meadows. Major Adam Stephen, covered with mud and blackened with powder, formed the Virginia Regiment up for the march. While he did, a French soldier pillaged his uniform from his baggage, but the Virginia major ran him down, seized his bag, "kicked the fellow's backside and returned." Two French officers protested that Stephen's actions violated the capitulation agreement, but he scoffed and "damned the capitulation and swore they had broke it already." The French officers asked "the dirty, half naked fellow" if he was an officer, which Stephen answered by opening his baggage and putting on his "flaming suit of laced Regimentals." The display of pomp and gusto by Stephen impressed the Frenchmen, who then told the Virginian that they wished to accompany him to Virginia as hostages, as they "understood there were a great many Belles Mademoiselle there."[150]

Washington recalled that although they marched away with the honors of war, the Natives plundered the British baggage, which was to have been left unmolested. De Villiers claimed that the British left in such haste that they abandoned one of their flags and banners. Apparently, British stragglers remained in the fort, and the French urged them to leave while they distracted the Indians, who wanted pillage and scalps. The French detachment then "went to work immediately and demolished the fort," burning it to the ground. Later, the Indians realized that they had lost out on their expected spoils from the battle and followed the column, capturing ten stragglers. De Villiers ordered the Indians to return them to Washington and sent a small escort of Frenchmen. The Indians feigned agreement and marched them away, only to strip them all naked and then kill and scalp three of them before leaving seven naked British with the French escorts. The French freed the survivors and then hurried back to Great Meadows with the Indians, who were "reprimanded." The Indians also captured at least eight other prisoners and took them back to Fort Duquesne, where they were on hand to greet Captains Stobo and Van Braam when de Villiers's force arrived.[151]

Washington's column covered only three miles, making slow progress, with the men having to carry the wounded and baggage. They halted to bivouac and establish a refuge for the wounded who could not make the journey to Wills Creek. He called roll, and the Virginia Regiment counted 293 men that July 4 evening. When they departed the next morning, he left the wounded and sick under the care of Dr. Craik and a detachment to await wagons to carry them back. The column slowly retreated to Wills Creek, where sixteen Virginians informed Washington that they had enlisted to obtain the land bounties, but recent events had altered their plans and they were quitting. Washington urged them to stay, promising to obtain rewards from Dinwiddie, but it was to no avail, as they departed anyway. Washington also received a letter dated July 5 from his friend William Fairfax belatedly warning him that the promised reinforcements would not be forthcoming, as George well knew. Fairfax, not knowing of the battle, cautioned Washington to "do little but guard, look out, and now & then bring in a straggling party of

These remnants of Fort Necessity survived the French burning of the stockade and were located by archaeologists deep in the wet earth. These and other similar remains allowed the current and accurate reconstruction of the fort. *Author photo.*

other ambassadors." Leaving the haggard force at Wills Creek, Washington and Mackay rode to Winchester, where they reported to Colonel Innes and encountered two of his North Carolina companies. They then traveled across Virginia to Williamsburg in the thick, humid summer heat, arriving on July 17. The recent experiences weighed heavily on George, and Captain Mackay observed that "Mr. Washington was very sad company."[152]

Meanwhile, the French destroyed Fort Necessity and then marched away from Great Meadows. On their return to Fort Duquesne, they halted briefly at Gist's settlement, burned it to the ground and then resumed their journey to the confluence of Redstone Creek and the Monongahela River. There they retrieved their canoes, destroyed the Ohio Company's storehouse and then embarked downstream, arriving at the Forks of the Ohio on July 7 with their mission accomplished. The British had been driven from the Ohio Country, and Jumonville had been avenged. Governor Duquesne received reports of the French success, ordered all offensive operations to halt and reduced manpower in the region to conserve supplies. Captain

Washington's Retreat from Fort Necessity, by Howard Pyle. *Boston Public Library.*

Louis Coulon de Villiers continued his service to the French Crown, leading guerrilla raids into Pennsylvania and fighting at Fort Oswego and Fort William Henry. For the latter, he earned the praise of General Louis-Joseph de Montcalm, and his actions gained him the Cross of St. Louis and admission into the knighthood of the Royal and Military Order of St. Louis. However, smallpox struck him shortly after receiving this honor, and he died in Quebec on November 2, 1757.[153]

In Williamsburg, Washington and Mackay provided Lieutenant Governor Dinwiddie a sanitized version of the affair at Great Meadows. The three men agreed that the nearly five hundred men from the New York Independent Companies and Innes's North Carolina command had failed to support Washington. On July 19, the *Virginian Gazette* published Washington and Mackay's after-action report and offered its own editorial on the situation: "Thus have a few brave men been exposed, to be butchered, by the negligence of those who, in obedience to the Sovereign's command ought to have been with them many month's before; and it is evidently certain, that

On July 4, 1754, victorious French troops pulled up most of Fort Necessity's white oak posts and piled them against what was left of the stockade. Then they lit it all on fire. Buried below ground, these post ends survived the blaze and were unearthed by archaeologist J. C. Harrington almost 200 years later.

Remnants of the posts from Fort Necessity's stockade found by archaeologists. These posts were below ground and survived the French burning. They and other sections of posts allowed for the accurate reconstruction of the fort that visitors see today. *Author photo.*

had the Companies from New York been as expeditious as Capt. Mackay's from South Carolina, our camp would have been secure from the insults of the French, and our brave men still alive to serve their King and Country."[154]

Dinwiddie believed that if the New Yorkers had arrived in a timely manner, "the French would not have attacked us, or if they had, if these Companies behaved with the valor and resolution of the others, in all probability, we should have defeated them." He considered the New Yorkers' delay "monstrous" and fumed that they "had nothing fit for a march or an engagement," bringing only one barrel of black powder. In Williamsburg, Washington found that the leading men of Virginia still held him in confidence, and they accepted that blame for his failure rested elsewhere. Perhaps Dinwiddie summed up the feeling in Virginia when he wrote to James Abercromby, "This affair gives me very great concern, but what can be done after such monstrous delays, few men and no money? It's of great consequence to the nation and these Colonies, that I think no time is to be lost, for if [the French] have a quiet settlement for two years, we shall never be able to root them out."[155]

While Dinwiddie publicly supported Washington, the governor's private correspondence reveals an effort to shield himself from any blame. To the Lords of Trade he wrote, "My Orders to Colo. W. were not to attack the Enemy 'till the other Forces had joined him, but the suddenness of the Information of the French marching to attack them, obliged our Forces to stand on the defensive." By July 31, Dinwiddie had focused his attention on Washington. To Governor Hamilton of North Carolina and Governor Sharpe of Maryland, he wrote that the action at Great Meadows "gave me much concern; my orders to the commanding officer were by no means to attack the enemy, till all the forces were joined in a body. They were surprised and had no account of their march till the morning before action."[156]

It was not long before others joined in the criticism of Washington. Governor Sharpe of Maryland concluded that Washington advanced recklessly into the Ohio Country and exposed his force to attack by an overwhelming French force. However true, it neglects consideration of the urgency that Dinwiddie had attached to Washington's expedition. The ambitious Washington knew little of military affairs, but he understood his orders and sought to comply with them and impress his patron and mentor to secure a career in the military. However true, such details mattered little in London. The Earl of Albemarle, the formal governor of Virginia and ambassador to France, accurately observed, "Washington and many such may have courage and resolution, but they have no knowledge or experience in our profession, consequently, there can be no dependence on them. Officers, and good ones, must be sent to discipline the militia and to lead them on as this nation, we may then (and not before) drive the French back to their settlements and encroach on them as they do at present upon us." For Washington, Albemarle's reference to the British military "profession," with its rules and regulations, certainly would have struck a nerve in the sensitive Virginian.[157]

Other colonial officials viewed Washington's defeat more in terms of the long-term outcomes that would arise. In New York, Goldsbrow Banyar, a key provincial official who held several important posts, read Washington and Mackay's published account of the battle and concluded, "I dare say when we hear the truth it will appear unfavorable enough on our side." He added, "It would be some consolation to us under this loss, might we depend on its raising in the Colonies a proper resentment, and put them upon raising supplies of men and money, but I fear this is rather to be wished for than expected." In reply, Sir William Johnston, New York's agent to the Iroquois and a veteran of King George's War, noted, "I have been always of opinion since I knew our weakness there [Ohio Country], that we should be banged by the French, and that would be attended by very bad consequences." Johnson wished that "Washington had acted with prudence and circumspection requisite in an officer of rank, and the trust at the same time reposed in him, but I can't help but saying he was very wrong in many respects.…I doubt his being too ambitious of acquiring all the honor or as much as he could before the rest joined him and giving too much credit to the reports or accounts given him by the French deserters (Which did not show him at all the soldier) was the rock on which he split. He rather should have avoided an engagement until all our troops were assembled for march in such a close country and by detachments will never do." In the larger picture, Johnson feared that the backcountry of the colonies would soon be exposed "to the ravages and cruelty of every little scalping party of French and Indians."[158]

Major Adam Stephen rushed to Washington's defense: "Let any of these brave gentlemen who fight so many successful engagements over a battle, imagine himself at the head of 300 men, and labor under the disadvantages afore mentioned, and would he not accept of worse terms as Col. Washington agreed to with all the honors of war, without mention of Assassination.…It appears to me, that if he did not, he might justly be said to be accessary to the destruction of so many men which would have been the consequence of his mistaken courage or obstinacy."[159]

News of the surrender and Washington's defeat at Fort Necessity reached London in early September. When the Duke of Cumberland, commander in chief of the British army, learned of it, he deemed it "a lamentable affair." When he read Washington's report, the duke was incredulous that one hundred Indians could effectively harass three hundred armed Virginians during the retreat.[160]

The terms of the capitulation, including the assassination reference, soon became a topic of controversy and Washington the object of derision. Washington and others immediately fixed blame on Van Braam, the interpreter. Major Stephen wrote shortly after the engagement:

When Mr. Van Braam returned with the French proposals, we were obliged to take the sense of them by word of mouth. It rained so heavily that he could not give us a written translation of them; we could scarcely keep the candle lit to read them. They were wrote in a bad hand, on wet and blotted paper, so that no person could read them but Van Braam, who had heard

*them from the mouth of the French officer. Every officer then present, is
willing to declare, that there was no such word as assassination mentioned;
the terms expressed to us were "the death of Jumonville."*[161]

While accepting responsibility for the "death of Jumonville" may have
been how it was explained, Washington did acknowledge accountability for
his demise, albeit without the dark connotations of an assassination. The
publication of Washington's journal by the French in 1757 resurrected
the issue of Washington admitting to the assassination of Jumonville, and
George lashed out at Van Braam. "We were willfully, or ignorantly, deceived
by our interpreter in regard to the word *assassination.*" Washington explained
that the interpreter "was a Dutchman, little acquainted with the English
tongue." Washington was certain of one thing: Van Braam referred to
Jumonville's demise as "the death or loss of Sieur Jumonville." Washington,
Mackay and the other officers subsequently learned otherwise, to their "great
surprise and mortification." As a result of the controversy, Van Braam was
omitted from the list of officers formally thanked by the Virginia House of
Burgesses. Sadly, the Dutchman languished in French captivity for several
years, but he subsequently received nine thousand acres of land as an officer
in the Virginia Regiment and a commission in the 60th Regiment of Foot,
the Royal Americans.[162]

The capture of Washington's journal also subjected Washington's record
of events to French scrutiny. When Governor Duquesne read a translation
of the journal, he crudely but somewhat accurately assessed of Washington
that "the hypocrisy of the Englishman is unmasked. That of the Five
Nations [Iroquois League] is no less uncovered, but after all the Englishman
is their dupe, because after so many pretty promises they abandoned him
at the moment when he had the most need of them." He added, "He lies
very much to justify the assassination of sieur de Jumonville…which he had
the stupidity to confess in his capitulation." While Washington downplayed
the accuracy of the French publication, the editors of his journals reviewed
a contemporary copy of the diary in Captain Contrecoeur's papers and
concluded that "the amount of deliberate French 'editing' of the journal
was probably less than historians have believed and was probably confined
to critical annotation and comments."[163]

Despite the criticism and failure, Washington would regain his footing.
Governor Horatio Sharpe of Maryland, the new commander of British
forces at Wills Creek, reassessed the situation. By early fall, he wanted to
keep Washington in the army and reassured him that after further reflection

on the matter (and after seeing the accounts of other "gentlemen who had been witnesses of the affair"), "I am not insensible of the difficulties you had to encounter, & I do not by the issue of that enterprise in the least measure the merit of the Gentlemen concerned therein." Sharpe prophetically told Washington, "I make no doubt, but your future behavior will convince the World of the injustice done you by the suspicions they have entertained." For Washington, that success did not come for many years, but when it did, he changed the world. Until then, July 3 would be a date he forever remembered the hard-learned lessons of war at Fort Necessity. Twenty-two years later, as the Revolutionary War moved toward an epic encounter with the British in New York, Washington wrote to Adam Stephen that he never let the anniversary of that formative event of July 3 pass "without a grateful remembrance of the escape we had at the Meadows" thanks to the mercies of "Providence."[164]

Chapter 8

"MORE EMPTY THAN THE COMMISSION ITSELF"

Washington Resigns

Despite Washington's failure, the determined Scotsman Robert Dinwiddie desperately planned a renewed campaign, for in his "humble opinion, no time is to be lost." In July, he ordered Colonel Innes to construct a "fort and magazine for stores and provisions" at Wills Creek that later became Fort Cumberland. Dinwiddie feared that if he waited until the spring of 1755, the French would strengthen their grasp on in the Ohio Country. On August 1, he informed Washington that the Virginia Council resolved that Washington "should immediately march over the Allegheny Mountains, either to dispossess the French of their Fort, or build a fort" at Redstone Creek on the Monongahela or "in a proper place" to be determined by a council of war. He further directed Washington to raise his regiment to three hundred men and march immediately with the complete companies on hand and leave orders for the others to follow when they reached sufficient manpower. He implored Washington to use his "usual diligence and spirit to encourage our people to be active on this occasion." Dinwiddie also directed the overall commander, Colonel Innes, to recruit the three Independent Companies then at Wills Creek to full strength. Despite the setback at Great Meadows, Dinwiddie planned to launch a second campaign and had already sent instructions to Colonel Innes. The governor also still retained confidence in Washington and directed Innes to "take the advice of Col. W" in filling vacant offices in the Virginia Regiment.[165]

By this this time, the Virginia Regiment had marched to Winchester in a demoralized state. Virginia had failed to pay the men their wages, and desertion ran rampant. Some even carried off their weapons when they went. Even worse, this occurred with the full knowledge of some officers. At Mount Vernon, Washington received accounts from Winchester and informed Dinwiddie of the deteriorating situation among the Virginians. The lieutenant governor replied, "I am sorry to hear your regiment have behaved so very refractory, though they have a right to their pay, they should have been easy till you returned." Dinwiddie concluded that the cause of the problem was "want of proper command." The lieutenant governor quickly shifted topics to a complaining resignation letter from Lieutenant Colonel George Muse. Dinwiddie responded that Muse "was welcome to resign," which he did, leaving Adam Stephen the regiment's new lieutenant colonel. Dinwiddie apparently sensed Washington's personal demoralization and reiterated his August 1 communication. "I repeat my orders now and am in hopes you will meet with little difficulty in complying therewith" and that he would soon be at Wills Creek with his regiment. But Dinwiddie's words fell on deaf ears. This probably dumbfounded Washington. He had been on his way to Redstone Creek when the French stormed after him. Furthermore, this was not the eager, compliant Washington of early spring 1754, for he was not just defeated at Fort Necessity—he was beaten, and his pride and youthful ego had yet to recover.[166]

On the same day, Dinwiddie wrote to Lieutenant Colonel Stephen, then in physical command of the regiment due to Washington's absence. He informed Stephen that the governor saw "no difficulty in raising men" and that he expected Stephen to march soon. He also informed John Carlyle in Alexandria of the plan "proposed and approved by the council." Once again, Carlyle was to supply the latest expedition and consult with Washington as to the needs in tools, powder and lead. He also ordered Captain Andrew Mountour to gather "as many of the young warriors of the Indians as you can" and take them to Wills Creek. These communications further highlighted Dinwiddie's inability to understand that regardless of orders from Williamsburg, the realities of the situation would prevent their successful fulfillment. Obtaining supplies was difficult—getting them to the troops was even harder. Indian allies were few before the debacle at Great Meadows, and their numbers had only lessened as a result.[167]

When Dinwiddie ordered a renewed campaign in late summer and fall, it overwhelmed the downtrodden Washington. The plan was based on unrealistic assumptions regarding logistics and manpower reflective of

Dinwiddie's failure to learn from their recent defeat. Washington, already dejected from his failure and the disintegration of his regiment after their unfulfilled exertions in the first campaign, could not fathom Dinwiddie's latest scheme. He wrote to his benefactor, William Fairfax, detailing Dinwiddie's exact orders and concluding, "Thus, Sir, You will see, I am ordered, with the utmost dispatch, to repair to Wills Creek with the Regiment: to do which under the present circumstances, is as impracticable as it is (as far as I can see the thing) to dispossess the French of their Fort, both of which, with our means, are morally impossible." The condition of the troops and Virginia's logistical failures alone should have precluded the attempt. In complaining to the influential Fairfax, Washington was working a back channel and hoped that Fairfax could dissuade Dinwiddie from his scheme.[168]

Washington wrote to Innes regarding the proposed campaign, but that communication has not been found. The North Carolinian had not yet received Dinwiddie's instructions for a renewed offensive written on August 1. His only orders thus far were to build the fort at Wills Creek and reorganize the troops. In the latter regard, Innes informed Washington that he hoped to cobble together a single company from the remnants of his disintegrated North Carolina command, another sign of Dinwiddie's misreading of the situation. The Scotsman believed that Innes's North Carolina command numbered 350 men. Innes revealed that he had arms, tents and ammunition for the Virginia Regiment at Winchester. Innes planned to travel to Wills Creek soon and looked forward to seeing Washington there, but he gave him no direct orders. Based on Washington's response to Innes on August 12, Washington initially planned to write to "Williamsburg" sharing his thoughts on the orders for a renewed campaign. Upon further reflection, he reconsidered and told Innes that George would wait until "you signify your sentiments to me on this head, that I may be guided thereby, and write nothing inconsistent with what you represent or advise." It was perhaps a moment of growth for George, as he recognized the need to align himself with his commanding officer and that the dire reality of the situation would ultimately end Dinwiddie's plans. He also assured Innes that if he ordered Washington to march to Wills Creek, he would do so even "if no more than ten men follows me (which I believe will be the full amount)."[169]

By August 15, reality began setting in on Governor Dinwiddie. He informed Henry Fox, the secretary of war, about the ordered expedition but noted that if it was found impractical, they would construct a fort "to facilitate operations of next spring." He cited the dearth of "experienced officers and military men in this part of the world" and the need for assistance from Great Britain for there to be any chance of success. He also requested that London send a strong and well-supplied force to Virginia. The Scotsman's hopes for a quick resumption of offensive activity in the Ohio Country were fading fast.[170]

The Virginia Regiment had returned to Alexandria by the middle of August, and its deterioration continued. Washington urged Dinwiddie of "the great necessity there is of a regulation of the soldiers' pay, and that a deduction be made for the Country to furnish them with clothes; otherwise, they will never be fit for service." The change of scenery did nothing to prevent desertions; while Washington and the officers were at church, twenty-five Virginians attempted to desert "but were stopped and imprisoned before the plot came to its full height." Washington desired strong measures to address discipline problems and requested formal guidance on a firm legal basis that he could use to conduct valid courts-martial, as "at this time, there is absolute necessity for it."[171]

On August 22, Dinwiddie dispatched Captain Alexander Finnie and an armed party to escort "the French prisoners, being one officer, two cadets, La Force, and 17 private men," to Colonel Innes at Wills Creek. However, Dinwiddie revoked the exchange of La Force and ordered Innes to return him to Williamsburg. The governor also informed Innes that "the disbanding [of] your regiment has greatly interrupted my former orders to you" and asked his opinion on what Innes could accomplish with the force at hand. By September 6, Dinwiddie's correspondence with others admitted, "I think with the small number of men we have, we cannot, this winter, venture over the Allegheny Mountains."[172]

Lieutenant William La Peronie recovered from his wounds and traveled to Williamsburg, where he sat in on the House of Burgesses. On September 5, he wrote to Washington of the latest developments on the political front. He noted that Washington would remain in command of the Virginia Regiment and incorrectly claimed that it would soon be increased to six hundred men and elevated to be part of the British military establishment. La Peronie also heard rumors that Lieutenant Colonel Muse had disparaged the officers of the Virginia Regiment, claiming that "he was bad but that the rest was as bad as he." Even worse, Muse had claimed that he challenged Washington to a fight, but the younger, bigger and stronger Washington backed down. When questioned on the veracity of Muse's claim, La Peronie replied that Muse would have been better off choosing to "go to hell than doing it [fighting Washington] for had he such thing declared, that this was his sure road." Muse's falsehoods angered La Peronie, who exclaimed, "Had I been in town at the time, I couldn't have helped to make use of my horse's whip for to vindicate the injury of that villain."[173]

Meanwhile, the failure of the Virginia House of Burgesses to fund Dinwiddie's renewed campaign to capture Fort Duquesne doomed any further effort in 1754. He notified Washington on September 11 and ordered him to take the Virginia Regiment to Wills Creek and report to Colonel Innes. The colonel, however, permitted Washington to wait until he had completed the recruitment of his regiment before ordering him to march, and Washington remained in Alexandria. Meanwhile, Dinwiddie had been corresponding with London, and it was determined that another effort should be made. King George II appointed Governor Horatio Sharpe of Maryland as Royal Commander in Chief of all British Forces and commander of colonial forces in the Virginia region, outranking Innes. Sharpe had served previously as a captain in the 20th Regiment of Foot during the Scottish Jacobite Rebellion and later served as a lieutenant colonel in the West Indies. That fall, Dinwiddie invited Sharpe and Governor Arthur Dobbs of North Carolina to Williamsburg, where the three men planned a renewed campaign to the Forks of the Ohio. Notably, they did not include Washington in the discussions. In a further turn of events, Dinwiddie broke the Virginia Regiment into independent companies, removing Washington's command. Dinwiddie claimed that the decision was made in London, but it was his choice.

Washington arrived in Williamsburg on October 19. While there, he received the thanks of the House of Burgesses for his efforts in the Ohio Country. When he learned of the decision to break his regiment into independent companies, the proud Virginian surrendered his commission on October 23. Whatever happened next, Washington was officially out of the military and turned his attention to the business and legal affairs at Mount Vernon.

Dinwiddie still hoped that Washington would reconsider his stance and enlisted Sharpe and William Fitzhugh to woo George back into the service. In early November 1754, Fitzhugh wrote to Washington and mentioned returning to his colonel's commission. He informed Washington that Governor Sharpe of Maryland had offered Washington his colonelcy with "honor and satisfaction." "I am very confident the General [Sharpe] has a very great regard for you," wrote Fitzhugh, "and will in every circumstance in his power make you very happy." Fitzhugh earnestly hoped that Washington continued in the military and advised him "by no means to quit." Still, the thought of service as Sharpe had offered offended George, and he expressed disappointment that Fitzhugh believed him "capable of holding a commission that has neither rank nor emolument annexed to it." He took offense that Fitzhugh even suggested staying on, writing, "You must entertain a very contemptible opinion of my weakness and believe me to be more empty than the commission itself." He viewed the decisions regarding the Virginia Regiment exclusively as a reflection on himself, when in fact Dinwiddie had many matters to consider. Washington also simmered over captains with a king's commission outranking colonial colonels. Internally, George wanted in on the action, but his pride would allow him to serve only under his terms. Although he resigned, he admitted, "My inclinations are strongly bent to arms."[174]

Chapter 9

"TO ATTAIN A SMALL DEGREE OF KNOWLEDGE ON THE MILITARY ART"

General Braddock's Campaign

I n 1755, the British Crown took control of the effort to drive the French from the disputed Ohio Country, while Dinwiddie still played an integral role in the colonies. Although no formal declaration of war was invoked, Major General Edward Braddock brought the 44th and 48th Regiments of Foot to Virginia, accompanied by a large train of artillery, totaling nearly 1,700 British Regulars. Colonial troops augmented the Regulars, increasing it to more than 2,000 men. Braddock's force included the Independent Companies that previously had been part of Washington's Virginia Regiment. After his resignation, he seemed destined to sit out the pending campaign. With this powerful force, Braddock intended to drive off the French and capture Fort Duquesne at the Forks of the Ohio.[175]

In March, a British fleet carrying Braddock's Regulars sailed up the Chesapeake Bay and the Potomac River, destined for Alexandria, then a fledgling port town. The ships churned through the choppy waters and cruised by Mount Vernon, where Washington managed his private business affairs with little expectation of a military commission or command. His opportunity for redemption of his military reputation figuratively slipped away as the ships moved out of sight, completing their voyage to Alexandria by the middle of the month. Surprisingly and unbeknownst to Washington, Braddock knew of the young Virginian and desired him to join the campaign as a staff officer. Washington's presence added the hands-on experience in the Ohio Country that Braddock sorely lacked.

To Washington's great surprise, Captain Robert Orme wrote to George at Braddock's behest. Orme noted Washington's prior resignation and aversion to a commission based "upon some disagreeableness that you thought might arise from the Regulation of command." Braddock, however, sought to smooth over those difficulties. Orme told Washington that the general "will be very glad of your company in his family by which all inconveniences of that kind will be obviated." Orme added that he would be quite pleased "to form an acquaintance with a person so universally esteemed," buoying Washington's spirits. It was an opportunity for George to redeem his reputation and learn military arts from British Regulars. However, as his noted biographer Douglas Southall Freeman pondered, "The Virginian had lost his small battles with mud and mountains and haggling farmers who would risk a war to save a wagon. Would these commanders from home show him where he had erred and how he might have won? Campaigning in the Ohio Country presented new challenges for these seasoned Brits and there were no guarantees of success."[176]

Despite the allure of Braddock's offer, Washington delayed accepting the commission, admitting his "selfish and sinister" views over rank. He informed Orme, "I want for noting more earnestly than to attain a small degree of knowledge on the Military Art." George also recognized that "a more favorable opportunity cannot be wished than serving under a Gentleman of his Excellency's known ability and experience." Although Washington was eager to join the staff as a volunteer, his business affairs at Mount Vernon, which he had leased recently from Lawrence's widow, presented one obstacle. Familial concerns also vexed George. When his mother learned that he was preparing to head off to the Ohio Country for another showdown with the French and their allies, she grew alarmed and traveled to Mount Vernon to dissuade him of this risky notion. Furthermore, he struggled to find someone to competently manage his business affairs in his absence. He eventually employed his younger brother, John Augustine "Jack" Washington. Despite these seemingly weighty issues at that moment, Washington informed Orme that he had "determined to do myself the honor of accompanying you," if the general would allow Washington additional time to put his business and familial affairs in order, which he did. George proudly explained to his associates that he served as a volunteer officer "in the Service of my country; to merit whose regard & esteem, is the sole motive that induces me to make this Campaign." Patriotism aside, he also made sure to accentuate his personal sacrifice, declaring that his service "will prove very detrimental to my private affairs as I leave a family scarcely

Braddock marker in Winchester containing an artillery piece that Braddock's army left in Alexandria when it departed for the campaign. *Author photo.*

settled, & in great disorder." Unlike in 1754, Washington no longer played the leading role in the Ohio Country. Although he was pleased with the prestige of serving as an aide on Braddock's staff, his stature clearly had diminished, and the days when he corresponded with Governor Dinwiddie and led troops into battle had vanished.

Before concluding his personal affairs and officially joining the staff, Washington visited Braddock at John Carlyle's regal stone house in Alexandria, Virginia, which the general had chosen as his headquarters. Carlyle soon discovered his new tenant to be "too fond of his passions, women and wine." George's new role on Braddock's staff exposed him to all the army's meetings, activities and decision making. On April 15, Braddock met with the governors of five colonies in what later became known as the Congress of Alexandria. They discussed funding and logistical considerations for his campaign against France in the colonies. The overall campaign included not only the primary focus against Fort Duquesne but also secondary offensives against Fort Niagara on Lake Ontario and Fort St. Frederic at Crown Point on the southern shore of Lake Champlain to pin down French forces. The meeting failed to deliver the support that Braddock expected from the colonies due to recalcitrant assemblies that did not fully support the Royal Governors' requests. Braddock bemoaned the lack of colonial support, saying, "I have been greatly disappointed by the neglect and supineness of the Assemblies of those provinces with which I am concerned, they promised great matters and have done nothing whereby instead of forwarding they have obstructed the service." The colonies' subsequent efforts as the campaign progressed did little to alter the general's opinion.[177]

While the meeting did not fulfill Braddock's expectations, it presented Washington with an unprecedented opportunity to meet five colonial governors. Governor William Shirley of Massachusetts in particular impressed George. Shirley's "character and appearance has perfectly charmed me," wrote Washington to William Fairfax. Shirley, an experienced and successful British officer in the previous war with France, now served as the British army's second in command in the colonies and would lead the efforts against New France in the northern colonies. His son William Shirley Jr. had already served as Braddock's military secretary since the fall of 1754 within the military "family" Washington was joining. In addition to the immediate staff, several other officers who would cross paths with Washington during the Revolution served on Braddock's expedition. Lieutenant Colonel Thomas Gage later served as commanding general of British forces in the colonies at the outset of the Revolutionary War. Horatio Gates, a captain of a New York Independent Company; Lieutenant Charles Lee of the 44th Regiment of Foot; and Adam Stephen fought under Washington as generals during that war, and all three saw their careers end in disgrace. Teamsters Daniel Morgan and Daniel Boone went on to achieve fame, the former leading riflemen during the Revolution, rising to general and winning a critical victory at the Battle of Cowpens in January 1781.[178]

After learning the details of Braddock's plans, Washington quickly realized that the same mountainous terrain and logistical shortcomings

Governor William Shirley of Massachusetts. *Miriam and Ira D. Wallach Division of Art, Prints, and Photographs, New York Public Library Digital Collections.*

that wrecked his 1754 campaign already threatened Braddock's effort. Braddock had sent his chief commissary, Sir John St. Clair, on a reconnaissance to assess the situation. Unfortunately, he greatly underestimated the length and ruggedness of the effort to cross the mountains to the Ohio River, and the resultant planning proved circumspect. Washington quickly recognized the flaw. Before departing Mount Vernon on April 23, he penned a farewell letter to William Fairfax at Belvoir. "I shall this day set out for Wills Creek where I expect to meet the General and to stay, I fear too long, as our march must be regulated by the movements of the train," he wrote, "which I am sorry to say, I think will be tedious in advancing, very tedious indeed, as answerable to the expectation I have long conceived, though few believed." Washington arrived at his Bull Skin Creek plantation in the lush Shenandoah Valley by April 28, although the journey killed one horse and disabled three others, forcing him to acquire new mounts. He rode out of Bull Skin on May 1, traveling more than thirty miles to Frederick, Maryland, where he caught up with Braddock, who was fuming over the very transportation issues that had vexed Washington. At Frederick, Braddock experienced the same logistical failures that had doomed Washington the previous spring. Braddock had marched half of his force through Maryland because Marylanders had convinced him that the farmers of that colony would support his effort with wagons if they traveled through the colony. St. Clair was supposed to have constructed a road to Fort Cumberland but failed in that regard. Furthermore, Braddock had departed Alexandria assured that 200 wagons and 2,500 horses would await him at Wills Creek, provided by the Virginia and Maryland Colonies. Instead, only a fraction of the needed transportation had arrived at the fort. Fortunately, Benjamin Franklin stepped forward and procured 1,500 packhorses and 150 wagons with teams from Pennsylvania. Washington informed his mother, "I fear we shall wait some time for a sufficient number of wagons to transport us over the Mountains." Although logistics bedeviled Braddock, Washington enjoyed his new role in supporting the general but not being directly accountable for its direction. He wrote, "I

British supply wagon at Fort Ligonier. *Author photo.*

am very happy in the General's Family as I am treated with a complaisant Freedom which is quite agreeable; so that I have no reason to doubt the satisfaction I proposed in making the Campaign."[179]

On May 2, George rode out of Frederick with Braddock and his staff. Washington listened as the general cursed the Maryland Colony for failing to deliver on its promises. He fumed over the folly of taking half the army through Maryland at St. Clair's recommendation and promise to construct a road to the fort, only to re-cross the Potomac and march through the Shenandoah Valley and Winchester to reach Fort Cumberland. Washington well knew from his personal travels the infeasibility of the politically chosen Maryland route. Now he privately took "infinite satisfaction" listening to Braddock "damning it very heartily."[180]

As the expedition progressed, Washington found himself visiting familiar grounds, such as Thomas Cresap's settlement at Oldtown. There, Washington had stopped briefly in 1754, and it was where he had his first exposure to Native American culture as a young surveyor. Now he was returning with a powerful British force. When Washington arrived at Wills Creek on May 10, he found it much changed from when he departed in the summer of 1754. Fort Cumberland had been constructed under the direction of Captain John Dagworthy of Maryland under Innes's tenure. Originally named Fort

Mount Pleasant in 1754 after a nearby height, one of Braddock's officers renamed it Fort Cumberland in 1755. Now it became the hub of activity as Braddock marshalled his forces for his move against Fort Duquesne. While stationed there, Washington wrote to John Carlyle in Alexandria on May 14, "We are then to proceed upon our tremendous undertaking of transporting the heavy Artillery over the Mountains, which I believe will compose the greatest difficulty in the Campaign." Furthermore, Washington recognized from his limited experience that logistical considerations could present constant delays for Braddock: "I see no prospect of moving from this place; as we have neither Horse nor Wagons enough, and no forage for them to subsist upon." Washington concluded that the planned diversionary attacks in the northern colonies would distract the French from Braddock's effort. As such, "any danger from the enemy I look upon as a trifling." However, in the late 1780s, Washington recalled that he "used every proper occasion... to impress the Genl, & the principal officers around him...to the mode of attack, which more than probably he would experience from the Canadian French, and their Indians on his March." Unfortunately, Braddock favored "regularity and discipline" and held his French and Indian opponents "in such absolute contempt" that any suggestions were in vain.[181]

Emmanuel Episcopal Church, Cumberland, Maryland. This church sits on the ramparts of Fort Cumberland, which can be seen running between the two large pictures in the middle of the image. *Author photo.*

On May 15, Braddock ordered Washington to Hampton, Virginia, to retrieve £4,000 sterling from John Hunter to fund the expedition. Furthermore, Braddock needed an additional £10,000 sterling within two months. Washington wrote ahead and asked Hunter to meet him in Williamsburg in the interest of saving time, but Dinwiddie informed him that Hunter was out of town. George arrived in Williamsburg on May 22 and met Hunter's partner, Mr. Belfour, who arrived with the funds. Washington returned to Winchester on May 27, expecting to meet a company of cavalry from Braddock to escort him and the coinage to Fort Cumberland. The promised escort failed to arrive, so he cajoled a local militia company to accompany him to the fort.

Washington learned that Sir John St. Clair had embarked on a road building venture with five hundred men. He followed much of Washington's route from 1754, improving and expanding it as they went. St. Clair established an advance camp on the Little Youghiogheny (Casselman) River. As June progressed, Braddock's army slowly moved westward through the mountainous terrain. As the army crawled ahead and supplies proved elusive, Braddock again fumed at the lack of support from the Americans and railed against them and their colonial governments. Washington challenged Braddock on the matter and wrote, "Instead of blaming the individuals as he ought, he charges all his disappointments to a public supineness, and looks upon the country, I believe, as void of both honor and honesty." In Braddock's letters to the British government, he described the colonials as "very indifferent men" and concluded that there was a "want of honesty and inclination to forward the service" and that they were "not to be depended on."[182]

Braddock grew impatient as the delays stymied the march. Intelligence reports from the north indicated that French reinforcements were en route though still distant from Fort Duquesne. Droughts lowered the river levels and slowed progress of the river-borne movement of French troops and material. Braddock realized that at his current slow pace of march, the reinforcements would reach the forks before he did regardless of the circumstances, rendering its capture even more difficult. As the middle of June passed, Braddock called Washington aside before a council of war at the Little Meadows encampment only thirty-five miles west of Fort Cumberland. He queried the Virginian's opinion on dividing the army and sending a fast-moving column of picked men ahead to capture Fort Duquesne. "I urged it in the warmest terms I was master of, to push on; if we even did it with a chosen detachment for that purpose, with such

Braddock's army on the march through the Allegheny Mountains. *Miriam and Ira D. Wallach Division of Art, Prints, and Photographs, New York Public Library Digital Collections.*

artillery and such other things as were absolutely necessary leaving the heavy artillery and other convoys with the remainder of the Army, to follow by slow and regular marches," wrote Washington to his brother in late June. Regardless of Washington's influence or lack thereof on the matter, Braddock adopted the measure and placed Colonel Peter Halkett in command of the flying column and Colonel Thomas Dunbar in charge of the slow-moving heavy column.[183]

As Washington offered his views to Braddock, sickness was overtaking his body. He had previously observed that several men, including a captain of one of the British regiments, had died and that many others were sick "with a kind of bloody flux." On June 14, Washington departed the camp at George's Creek and was soon "seized with violent fevers and pains in my head which continued with intermission." The "violent" nature of his illness precluded him from riding his horse, so the orderlies placed him in a covered wagon that conveyed him toward Braddock's main army. However, the jolting proved too much for Washington to endure, so he abandoned the wagon and remained behind with a guard and some supplies to await the arrival of Dunbar's column. Washington despaired of missing the capture of Fort Duquesne, but Braddock assured him that Washington would be brought up before the army reached the French fort. However, the doctors feared that if

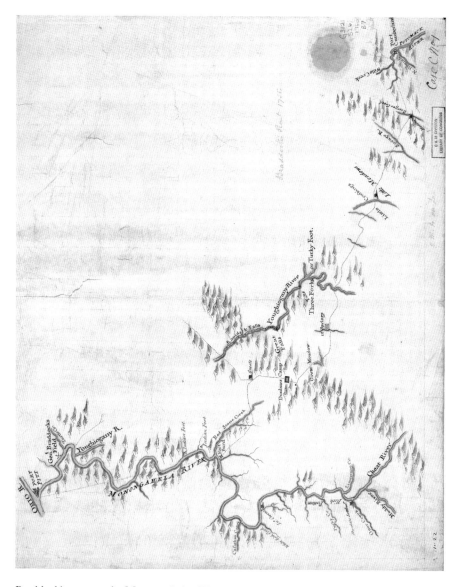

Braddock's route to the Monongahela. *Library of Congress.*

he exerted himself in his current condition, "it would endanger my life."[184] Roger Morris of Braddock's staff informed the ailing Washington, "It is the desire of every particular in the Family, & the Generals positive commands to you, not to stir, but by the Advice of the Person under whose care you are, till you are better, which we all hope will be soon."[185]

After a healthy dose of Dr. James' Powders, ordered by Braddock, Washington emerged from his fever and delirium and slowly regained some strength. He traveled in a covered wagon with Dunbar's lumbering column until he regained enough energy to ride. "Tho much reduced and very weak mounted his horse on cushions," Washington rejoined Braddock on July 8 as the army neared Fort Duquesne and found his military family debating its options for capturing the French bastion at the forks. At Braddock's headquarters tent that evening, Sir John St. Clair suggested that he personally lead a rapid night march to the French fort and deploy troops in front of it before the French could react to the English presence. St. Clair intended to bottle the French up in their fort so that they could not attack Braddock en route to the fort. In the end, Braddock rejected St. Clair's proposal. Instead, the advanced column remained concentrated and, on the advice of guides, would twice cross the Monongahela River at reliable fords where the river was shallow and low banks did not hinder the army's entering and exiting the water. This route avoided a difficult defile known as the "narrows," which would isolate the column between the bank of the Monongahela on the left and a steep height on the right, prime ground for a French and Indian ambush.[186]

Braddock's three-hundred-man vanguard led by Lieutenant Colonel Thomas Gage broke camp at 2:00 a.m. on July 9. The tall grenadiers of the 44th and 48th Regiments, "the best soldiers, unfrightened of adversity," followed veteran frontiersmen George Croghan down to the drought-shriveled Monongahela River, lugging two six-pounder guns for artillery support. Two hours later, Sir John St. Clair led his two-hundred-man working party, clearing a road down to the river crossing. At 5:00 a.m., Braddock broke camp with the balance of his army. By 9:30, Gage's vanguard had forded the river for the second time opposite the point where Turtle Creek joins the Monongahela from the east. This was familiar turf for Washington. He had twice visited Frazier's cabin on Turtle Creek during his 1753 voyage to the French forts. By noon, Braddock's army was well on its way, crossing "over the river in the greatest order with their bayonets fixed, Colors flying, and Drums and Fifes beating and playing, as they supposed the Enemy would take a view of them in the crossing." Music echoed off the mountains and reverberated throughout the valley. Washington described the scene as "the most beautiful spectacle he ever beheld." With the river crossings behind them, Braddock's men believed that they had "surmounted our greatest difficulties" and believed that the French "never would dare to oppose us." Confidence was high as they traversed the last leg of their journey to Fort Duquesne.[187]

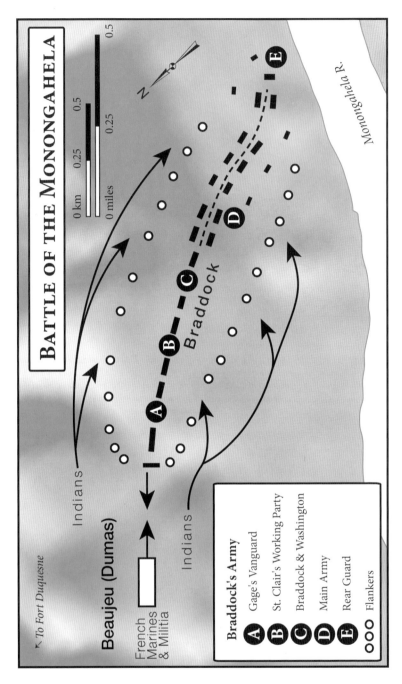

Battle of the Monongahela, based on the 1755 Patrick Mackellar map *A Sketch of the Field of Battle of the 9th of July Upon the Monongahela. Map by George Chakvetadze.*

Looking upstream on the Monongahela River at Braddock, Pennsylvania. Braddock's army made its final crossing of the river early on the morning of July 9, 1755, descending from the modern Kennywood amusement park on the right bank of the river and crossing over immediately downstream from its confluence with Turtle Creek. *Author photo.*

While Braddock marched toward the Forks of the Ohio, the French had not been idle. Captain Daniel Beaujeu had recently reinforced Captain Contrecoeur at Fort Duquesne. He brought with him not only 240 troops but also a reputation for bravery and an established relationship with their Indian allies. With Captain Contrecoeur ailing and unable to take the field, he appointed Beaujeu to command a force dispatched to strike Braddock's column. The assembling force included "2 captains, 4 lieutenants, 6 ensigns, 23 cadets, 72 men of the Regular troops, 146 militia, and 637 Indians" for a total of 891 men to strike Braddock's 1,400 as they crossed the Monongahela River.[188]

Inside the fort, the French and their Indian allies made final preparations for their ambush. The fort's commissary officer opened his stores to their native allies, who stocked up on flints, leaden musket balls, powder and other accoutrements. Captain Beaujeu went to confession with the fort's priest and performed his daily devotional prayers before turning to military matters. By 8:00 a.m., Beaujeu had marshalled the large force that had gathered on the ground outside Fort Duquesne and led them northeasterly along an old Indian trail that followed the Allegheny River to Shannopin's town. There they turned to the southwest and headed toward the confluence of Turtle Creek and the Monongahela River "on a direct collision course with Braddock's army." Beaujeu deployed Indian scouts in advance of his force who soon reported back that Braddock had crossed the river and was marching in column through the woods. They also provided precise dispositions of the British force, including the grenadiers, artillery and wagons.[189]

With this detailed information in hand, Beaujeu arranged his force for battle. He divided it up by the different Indian tribes and placed an officer who spoke their language at the head of each grouping. Many French officers dressed as their native allies did, wearing only gorgets as they led their men into battle. He advanced these detachments forward on both flanks concealed in the woods and ordered them to reveal themselves only when he had attacked the advanced British grenadiers with French Marines and militia.

The woods through which Gage's advance party and the scouts moved were so open that Sir John St. Clair declared, "The carriages could have been drove in any part of it." The first signs of trouble came when one of the mounted guides in the vanguard shouted, "The Indians are upon

"Braddock's Battlefield," engraving by A.W. Graham. *From Winthrop Sargent's* The History of an Expedition Against Fort Duquesne in 1755 *(1856).*

us." Harry Gordon, a British engineer, galloped ahead and joined George Croghan, where they had "free sight of the enemy as they approached." They saw only the small center element of Beaujeu's attacking force, with French officers in uniform and others dressed as Indians leading three hundred men forward. Gordon recalled seeing a French officer "at the head of them dressed as an Indian, with his gorget on, waved his hat, and they immediately dispersed to the right and left, forming a half-moon." Some Grenadiers grew unsteady upon hearing the guides shout warnings and retreated toward Gage, but officers quickly stifled the disorder. Gage shouted, "Fix your bayonets," deployed them into line of battle and charged toward the approaching French.[190]

The British arrived at the brow of a ravine overlooking the low ground where the French were moving at that moment. The grenadiers fired a volley down on the French, who returned a ragged blast of their own. The heavy fire from the grenadiers shook the French detachment, and Gage's two six-pounder cannons spewed their iron balls at the French. The British fire heavily damaged the French, who absorbed most of their casualties during this phase of the battle. The grenadiers surged ahead, shouting, "God Save the King," driving the French back in confusion. With artillery booming and the imposing British grenadiers closing in, many French militiamen ran off, along with a few Indians. In the ravine, Beaujeu feverishly rallied the men who did not run off, mostly Marines, when the British fired another volley that killed the French commander. Despite this weighty loss, the French attack regained its footing. Subordinate commanders Captain Jean-Daniel Dumas and Captain François-Marie Marchand de Lignery successfully rallied the men, but Beaujeu's original deployment of Indians struck the unsuspecting British flanks, quickly changing the course of battle. Dumas, now the senior commander, assumed overall command for the French.

Despite initial French troubles at the front, their Indian allies surged around the British flanks in a "kind of running fight," attacking Braddock's men from the sides where they were most vulnerable. They quickly overwhelmed the British flank guards and then struck the Gage's force. Hit on the flanks, the British could not bring their powerful massed musket fire to bear against the attackers. Gordon reported, "As soon as the Enemy's Indians perceived our Grenadiers, they divided themselves and ran along our right and left flanks." The war cries of the Indians pierced the woods and terrified the British troops. A commissary officer wrote, "The yell of the Indians is fresh on my ear, and the terrific sounds will haunt me until the hour of my dissolution." Another described it as a "violent horrid scream, perhaps the most horrid

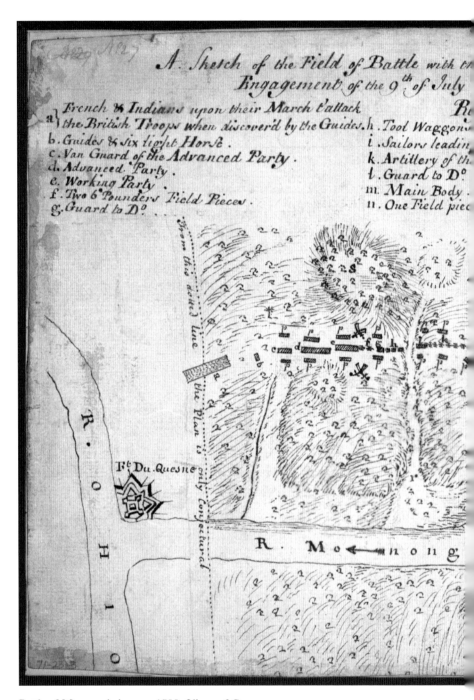

Battle of Monongahela map, 1755. *Library of Congress.*

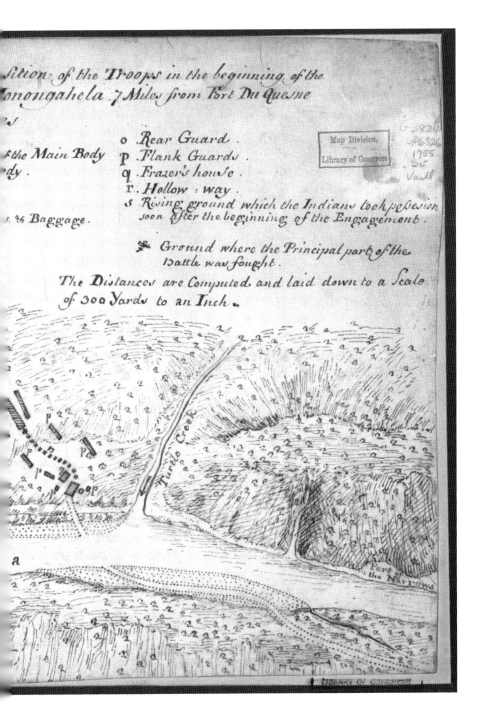

...sition of the Troops in the beginning of the
...ononygahela 7 Miles from Fort Du Quesne

o . Rear Guard .
...f the Main Body   p . Flank Guards .
...dy .   q . Frazer's house .
r . Hollow way .
s . Rising ground which the Indians took pofsefion
soon after the beginning of the Engagement .
...s . & Baggage .

✱ . Ground where the Principal part of the
Battle was fought .

The Distances are Computed and laid down to a Scale
of 300 Yards to an Inch.

sound that can be imagined." The French-aligned Indians "advantageously posted themselves behind trees, fired their discharge (a discharge all the more terrible as their fire was continual), and as you know, dear cousin, no shot of theirs is ever false." Officers ordered men into line of battle, faced them in the direction where they believed the threat originated and then ordered them to fire a volley. By the time the soldiers maneuvered and fired in unison, the Indians had shifted their position. Often the confused British fired into their own troops, adding to the horror. Braddock's army rapidly disintegrated under the accurate fire from the Indians on his flanks, and his vaunted Regulars panicked. Many Frenchmen who had retreated before the British grenadiers at the outset of the battle now rejoined the fight as the attack on the British flanks prevented the grenadiers from capitalizing on their brief success.[191]

General Braddock boldly galloped into the lethal cauldron of death. St. Clair, bleeding profusely from a wound, yelled out, "For God-sake to gain the rising ground on our right to prevent our being totally surrounded." Washington followed his commander into the fray, bearing orders to subordinate commanders amid the well-directed lethal crossfire that quickly took a heavy toll on Braddock's staff. One shot killed Shirley, and Robert Orme and Roger Morris went down wounded early in the engagement. Washington found "the duty hard upon me, as I was the only person then left to distribute the general's orders, which I was scarcely able to do, as I was not half recovered from a violent illness." As he dashed about the battlefield carrying Braddock's orders under a hail of musketry and the confusion of the flank attack, he noted that the British officers "behaved with incomparable bravery, for which they greatly suffered, there being near 60 killed and wounded, a large proportion of the number we had!" However, the "dastardly behavior of the English soldiers exposed all those who were inclined to do their duty to almost certain death." Conversely, Washington proudly observed several companies of Virginians from his former regiment who "behaved like men and died like soldiers," fighting on the army's right flank. While Washington's perspective on the Regulars is understandable given his personal observations, he failed to identify the French and Indian tactics that placed Braddock's force in a viselike trap, attacking both flanks and inflicting a 67 percent casualty rate on the British, as the proper cause for the soldiers' behavior.[192]

As the situation collapsed, Washington begged Braddock's permission to lead the Virginians into the woods and engage the French and Indians in woodland fashion "before it was too late." Braddock demurred at

Washington statue on Monongahela Battlefield, located on Jones Avenue in Braddock across the street from Fairless Elementary School at 531 Jones Avenue. *Author photo.*

the suggestion of frontier tactics, deeming it inappropriate until it was "too late for execution." British Regulars requested permission to shelter and fight behind trees like their stealthy opponents, but the inflexible Braddock refused any deviation from established procedures, and amid the crisis, he called them cowards for asking. With the lead balls ripping through the air, Washington narrowly avoided death or injury in the heart of the battle. The fire of the Indians left four bullet holes in his coat and one through his hat and knocked two horses out from under him. He fervently believed that only "the all-powerful dispensations of Providence" had saved him from death on the Monongahela.[193]

That same Providence did not extend its hand of protection to General Braddock. He and Washington desperately attempted to rally the shattered army, but the troops fled "like sheep before the hounds" as the Indians rapidly and accurately fired from the woods on the flanks. Washington recalled that their attempts to rally the troops "was with as little success as if we had attempted to had attempted to stop the wild bears of the mountains or rivulets with our feet, for they break by in spite of every effort that could be made to prevent it." Bringing up reinforcements, Braddock attempted to dislodge the Indians from an eminence on his right flank but only succeeded in taking heavy losses in the effort. Braddock personally rallied the men to make another effort in that direction when his fourth horse of the day was shot out from under him. No sooner did he climb atop a fifth than lead missiles ripped through his arm and into his chest, hurling him to the ground. Washington, Gage and Captain Robert Stewart, commander of the mounted Virginians serving as Braddock's escort, rushed to the fallen general's side. They removed his red sash, placed the stricken Braddock on it as a stretcher and carried him rearward. Eventually, Washington placed him in a tumbrel cart. As they navigated a confused sea of panicked soldiery, Braddock begged them to leave him on the battlefield to die, but they refused to abandon the general. Fortunately, the attacking Indians' fixation on scalping the hundreds of dead

Mortal wounding of Braddock at the Battle of the Monongahela. Photograph of portrait at Braddock's Battlefield History Center. *Author photo, 2016.*

and wounded and securing plunder from the battlefield allowed Braddock's party and many British to escape who otherwise could have been surrounded and captured.[194]

At the river, Washington and a few officers removed the stricken general from the cart and carried him across. Braddock then ordered Washington to ride ahead and rally men who had retreated farther down the road. He dashed toward the second ford, splashed through the water and ascended a hill, where he found Gage already performing the task Braddock had ordered. He delivered the orders, turned around, galloped back and reported his findings to the general. By then the sun had gone down, as darkness enveloped the scene. Braddock next directed the sick and weary Washington to ride to Colonel Dunbar and "make arrangements for covering the retreat and forwarding on provisions and refreshments to the retreating and wounded soldiery." Although "wholly unfit for the execution of the duty" from the "fatigues and anxiety of the last 24 hours," Washington and two guides traveled more than fifty miles through the "impervious darkness" of night rendered blacker by the "close shade of thick woods." At some places, Washington's guides could not see their way, dismounted their horses and felt along the ground to locate the road. The journey took all night and part of the next morning before Washington reached Dunbar's camp, a short distance from his fateful engagement with Jumonville. As Washington traveled, he encountered "the dead— the dying—the groans—lamentations—and cries along the road of the wounded for help were enough to pierce the heart of the adamant."[195] At Dunbar's camp, Washington finally rested and thanked Providence for his survival from a battle where nearly seven out of ten men were killed or wounded on the spot. He later confided to his younger brother, John Augustine or Jack, that he had survived the slaughter "by the miraculous care of Providence that protected me beyond all human expectation."[196]

Even before his arrival, panicked stragglers had already told Dunbar wild tales of the woe that had befallen Braddock on the Monongahela. As a result, a panic overcame Dunbar's command, and many deserted and headed east, so he posted sentries to stop it. Meanwhile, Braddock's fragmented command struggled through the night over the same route that Washington had taken. Survivors fashioned a makeshift stretcher, and six men lugged Braddock over the hilly terrain until they reached Gist's settlement at 10:00 p.m. on July 10. Although direly wounded, Braddock thought of his suffering men and ordered his commissaries to leave food behind at intervals along the road to feed the stragglers. They struggled up

The mortally wounded Braddock, taken from the Monongahela Battlefield in a tumbrel cart. Engraving by Alonzo Chappel. *Library of Congress*.

Tumbrel cart used to carry equipment and supplies at Fort Ligonier. *Author photo*.

Artifacts from Dunbar's camp at the Jumonville Retreat Center, Hopwood, Pennsylvania. These items were destroyed or abandoned during Dunbar's hasty withdrawal after Braddock's defeat. *Author photo.*

Chestnut Ridge and arrived at Dunbar's camp the next day. The sight of the dazed remnants of Braddock's once proud army straggling into camp stunned Dunbar's men, who themselves were still in a state of shock. On July 12, Braddock ordered a retreat to Fort Cumberland. The lack of transport for both the wounded and arms and supplies quickly became apparent. To make room for the wounded, Braddock ordered Dunbar to destroy all ammunition, mortars, cannons and anything that could not be taken with the army. Braddock determined that the French would not have any further gains at his expense.[197]

For Braddock, the reality of this shocking disaster finally emerged from his shock. His aide Captain Robert Orme noted that he remained quiet the day after the battle, but on July 11, he spoke, amazed at the events that had transpired. "Who would have thought it," he asked Orme before reverting to his stunned silence. A day later, the dying general asserted, "We shall better know how to deal with them another time." Sadly, Washington had offered guidance on the matter, and the rigid general rejected it in favor of traditional European tactics. Braddock's medical situation degenerated significantly,

Burial of Braddock, with Washington, Lieutenant Colonel Thomas Gage and Captain Horatio Gates in attendance, by Howard Pyle. *Boston Public Library.*

Original grave site of General Edward Braddock, in a trace of the Braddock Road. Washington had the army march over the spot afterward to conceal its location from pursuing Indians. *Author photo.*

and he proved unable to command. He resigned command of the army, and Dunbar led the march out of his camp on July 13. Braddock expired that evening a short distance west of the Great Meadows. With the dearth of officers after the battle, Washington assumed responsibility for arranging the general's burial. He later recalled:

> *The brave but unfortunate General Braddock breathed his last....Thus died a man whose good and bad qualities were intimately blended. He was brave even to a fault and in regular service would have done honor to his profession—His attachments were warm—his enmities were strong—and having no disguise about him, both appeared in full force. He was generous and disinterested—but plain and blunt in his manner even to rudeness.*[198]

Washington oversaw the burial of General Braddock the following morning. With Gage, Gates and other officers in attendance, Washington read funeral prayers over the general in a private ceremony and had his

remains interred under Braddock's Road to conceal it from the Indians and potential desecration. The entire army, with all its wagons, then passed over the grave "to hide every trace by which the entombment could be discovered." Washington described it as guarding "against a savage triumph."[199]

The army next passed Great Meadows, the scene of Washington's defeat at Fort Necessity and the beginning of his first retreat a little over one year prior. When he marched away in 1754, the downtrodden Washington probably didn't think that things could get worse, but in 1755 they did—he was now living through it. They crossed the Youghiogheny River at Great Crossing

Opposite: Braddock Road trace, near his grave and monument. *Author photo.*

Left: Braddock's grave and monument, part of the Fort Necessity National Battlefield. *Author photo.*

on July 15. Colonel Dunbar assigned Washington command of seventy men to escort lightly wounded officers and men to Fort Cumberland ahead of the main army. Among the stricken were Washington's associates from Braddock's "military family," Robert Orme and Roger Morris, for whom the young Virginian arranged the best care that the circumstances permitted. To ease their suffering, he had them carried on stretchers between two horses instead of riding in the jostling wagons over the rugged road. Before Washington reached Fort Cumberland, the panicked teamsters had arrived and spread their dire tales of the defeat to Colonel James Innes, the post commander. Innes, in turn, promptly relayed the message to Robert Dinwiddie, who replied that the news "gave me much grief and great concern for the defeat of our forces." The governor hoped that "it is not so bad as reported to you." Ever the optimist, Dinwiddie naïvely added, "As I hear Colonel Dunbar's Regiment was not in the engagement, if so, his coming up with fresh men might probably make a turn in our favor." Dunbar did not linger at Fort Cumberland; instead, he determined to march to Philadelphia and enter winter quarters in August. This movement frustrated the governor, who once more was already looking to launch another campaign for Fort Duquesne.[200]

Washington remained at Wills Creek for several days to regain the strength that illness and the exertions of the battle and its aftermath had sapped from his body. At Fort Cumberland on July 18, Washington promptly wrote to his mother that he was alive and safe. He stated that although Braddock had "1,300 well-armed troops," three hundred French and Indians defeated him because the British Regulars panicked when attacked in backwoods fashion. He also claimed that the confused British fired into their own men, causing most of their casualties. He praised the efforts of the gallant officers who suffered horrible losses and lamented his Virginians. Although unhurt, George explained, "I am still in a weak and feeble condition which induces me to halt here 2- or 3-days in hopes of recovering a little strength to proceed homewards." He followed that correspondence with a remarkably similar missive to Lieutenant Governor Dinwiddie. George added the startling news that Dunbar "intends so soon as his men are recruited at this place to continue his march to Philadelphia into *Winter* Quarters." This left Virginia's frontier virtually undefended except for the remnant of the Virginia companies. "I tremble at the consequences that this defeat may have upon our back settlers, who I suppose will leave their habitations unless there are proper measures taken for their security." Apparently tired of writing, he next penned a summarized version of affairs to his brother Jack.[201]

On July 22, George mounted his steed and departed Fort Cumberland. He traversed the mountains and ventured back to Virginia, headed for his beloved Mount Vernon. He followed the familiar route through the Shenandoah, reaching Winchester on the July 24, crossing the Blue Ridge at Vestal's Gap and passing through Loudoun County. He arrived at Alexandria on July 26. As Washington rode up the path to Mount Vernon on the Potomac River, the natural beauty and security of home provided the much-fatigued Washington with relief. William Fairfax of Belvoir rejoiced at his neighbor's safe return from the debacle on the Monongahela. "We have been in torturing suspense," he told George. "Now you are by a kind Providence preserved and returned to us." Fairfax requested that Washington "kindly invite us over, rightly judging our curiosity wants to be informed of some particulars." The ladies of Belvoir longed to visit the handsome hero, including Sally Fairfax, with whom Washington had long been smitten, although she was the wife of his friend George Fairfax. His heart surely fluttered when she wrote, "After thanking Heaven for your safe return, I must accuse you of great unkindness in refusing us the pleasure of seeing us this night." She added, "If you will not come to us tomorrow morning very early, we shall be at Mount Vernon." George was home and among friends after three months in the wilderness, where he experienced dire illness and the most horrid battle scenes in which the English had ever taken part in North America. At last, the refinements of civilization were at hand, but how long George enjoyed them remained an open question. The Battle of the Monongahela and Braddock's Campaign left an indelible impression on Washington. Shortly after returning, he told a friend, "When this story comes to be related in future Annals, it will meet with unbelief and indignation; for had I not been witness to the fact on that fatal day, I should scarce have given credit to it even now."[202]

Chapter 10

"IT WOULD REFLECT DISHONOR UPON ME TO REFUSE IT"

Washington Takes Command

Shortly after Washington's arrival at Mount Vernon on July 26, a letter from Dinwiddie arrived. Having only recently accepted the reality of Braddock's disaster and still shaken by the news, Dinwiddie asked George, "But pray Sir with the number of men remaining, is there no possibility of doing something [on] the other side of the mountains before the Winter months." It echoed the same theme that Dinwiddie had chosen on the heels of Washington's defeat at Great Meadows. The governor also doubted Washington's correct assertion that Dunbar would go into winter quarters in midsummer. "Surely you must mistake," the lieutenant governor wrote. He refused to believe that Dunbar could leave "his Majesty's Colonies…exposed to the invasions of the Enemy, no! He is a better officer & I have a different opinion of him." Dinwiddie remained wrapped in the misguided hope that Washington had erred regarding Dunbar. "I shall wait with impatience an answer to my letter to him."[203]

In Williamsburg, desperate officials clamored for Washington to resume his military career upon hearing exaggerated tales of his heroism on the Monongahela. He informed his older brother Augustine, who represented Westmoreland County in the Virginia House of Burgesses, that he had declined the invitation due to health, "so much has a sickness of five weeks continuance reduced me." Notably, he did not close the door on future service. "I can nevertheless assure you, and others that I am so little dispirited at what has happened, that I am always ready, and always willing to do my Country any services that I am capable of," he declared, "but never upon the terms I have done, having suffered much in my private fortune and impairing one of the best of constitutions." He next summarized his brief military career and his feelings on it:

> *I was employed to go on a journey in the Winter (when I believe few or none would have undertaken it) and what did I get by it? My expenses borne! I then was appointed with trifling pay to conduct a handful of men to the Ohio. What did I get by this? Why, after putting myself to the considerable expense in equipment and providing necessaries for the campaign—I went out, was soundly beaten, lost them all—came in, and had my commission taken from me or in other words my command reduced, under pretense of an order from home. I then went out a Volunteer with General Braddock and lost all my horses and many other things but this being a voluntary act I should not have mentioned it was it not to show that I have been upon the losing order ever since I entered the service, which is now near two years; so that I think I can't be blamed, should I, if I leave my family again, enter to do it upon such terms as to prevent my suffering.*[204]

Nevertheless, from this self-centered fledgling officer emerged the self-sacrificing leader of the Continental army during the American Revolution.

Other influential Virginians considered Washington a hero at the Battle of Monongahela and promoted his interest in the military. Philip Ludwell, a member of the Governor's Council, informed Washington that Dinwiddie had responded favorably to the suggestion that George receive command of the 1,200 men recently authorized by the House of Burgesses. "We could be so happy as to have you here at this time," wrote Ludwell, "and that it were known you were willing to take such a command." Cousin Charles Lewis informed George, "I think 'tis unanimously agreed, you shall command our forces in the next scheme to be executed." He added, "The people in these parts seem very desirous of serving under the brave Col. Washington, and want nothing more to encourage 'em out, but your declaration of going to command them." Clearly, the elites of Virginia had endorsed Colonel George Washington to lead the reconstituted Virginia Regiment, but he remained cautiously distant.[205] Virginia counted on Washington if for no other reason than a lack of other candidates with his standing and experience, however brief and wanting in success.

Washington was not yet ready resume command. As he noted to Warner Lewis on August 14, "Was I to have the command, I should insist upon some things which ignorance and inexperience made me overlook before, particularly that of having the Officers in some measure appointed with my advice and with my concurrence." Experience had taught George that he would be accountable for the actions of his subordinates and that if he were to fail on their account, he would go down with men of his choosing. On that same day, he wrote to his mother regarding his intentions during those tumultuous times: "If it is in my power to avoid going to the Ohio again, I shall, but if the Command is pressed upon me by the general voice of the Country, and offered upon such terms as can't be objected against, it would reflect dishonor upon me to refuse it; and that I am sure must, or ought, to give you greater cause of uneasiness than my going in an honorable Command; for upon no other terms I will accept."[206]

On that same day, Dinwiddie commissioned Colonel George Washington to command the reconstituted Virginia Regiment "with full Power & Authority to appoint all Officers both Civil & Military within the same." The new commission also met his financial demands, paying thirty shillings per day, £100 pounds per year for expenses and a 2 percent commission on all purchases he made in fulfillment of his duty. He later considered this an "enlarged and dignified commission" that met his expectations, but he did not immediately accept. On August 31, George Mason wrote to Washington hoping that the new commission would prove acceptable. Washington followed the advice of Werner Lewis and traveled to Williamsburg to make final arrangements, arriving on August 27. There remained but a single sticking point: Dinwiddie had already appointed the sixteen captains of companies—unacceptable for Washington. As a compromise, Dinwiddie allowed him to appoint the field officers. Even more convincing was perhaps the pressure exerted by influential Virginians that convinced George that he stood to lose more in terms of reputation and stature in Virginia if he refused the offer than by accepting the command without being able to appoint the captains. By early September, he relented and accepted the commission as commander in chief of Virginia's military forces.[207]

In the selection of field officers, he promoted veteran of the Fort Necessity and Braddock campaigns Adam Stephen to his former position of lieutenant colonel. He remained in charge of the remnant of the Virginians from Braddock's campaign stationed at Fort Cumberland. The experienced Andrew Lewis, a captain under Washington in 1754, now became the new major with the duty of organizing the newly raised companies at Winchester. Captain George Mercer, wounded at Fort Necessity as a lieutenant, became Washington's aide-de-camp. Thomas Waggener, wounded at Jumonville Glen and on the Monongahela, received a captain's commission. Ensign

George Weeden of Fredericksburg later became a general under Washington during the American Revolution. Sadly, several Washington favorites, such as captains William La Peronie and William Polson, died in combat on the Monongahela. Washington next traveled to Fredericksburg to meet his commissary, Charles Dick, who was absent. So, George left orders for him to provide supplies for the new companies being recruited. Fredericksburg, Alexandria and Winchester served as assembly points for the new units, and Washington expected Dick to supply their needs at the expense of Virginia. Washington also directed Dick to provide a barrel of gunpowder for Major Andrew Lewis so that the men could live fire their muskets during training. Washington had seen inexperienced men suffer and die on the frontier and now took innovative (at the time) and uncommon measures to prepare them.

Although Dinwiddie had hoped for a quick resumption of an offensive to capture Fort Duquesne, the reality of the situation dissuaded him of that notion. After Braddock's defeat, French-allied Indian war parties raided the western frontier settlements of Virginia, Maryland and Pennsylvania.

Colvin's Fort, Frederick County, Virginia. While sporting the title of fort, this structure at best served as a rallying point for area residents in the event of a raid during the war. *Author photo.*

Small parties struck isolated settlers, killing and scalping or capturing the inhabitants and destroying their homesteads. Able-bodied prisoners were carried back as war booty to become adopted into the tribes or taken to the French for rewards. If a prisoner proved unable to make the journey or hindered the rapid movement of the party, the Indians simply killed them. These raids panicked the backcountry settlers, who streamed eastward to safer and more populated areas.

Protecting Virginia's western settlements proved a nearly impossible task. "The frontiers were continually harassed," he recalled, "but not having force enough to carry the war to the gates of Fort Duquesne, he could do no more than distribute the troops along the frontiers in stockaded forts." Even then, the forts proved difficult to man and supply and did little to stop the actual raids. In the best-case scenario, they provided the locals a sense of security and served as a rallying point for the settlers when raids occurred.

For the next three years, Washington spent much time in Winchester, county seat of Frederick, in the northern Shenandoah Valley. It was an area he knew well from his time there as a surveyor. Germans and Scots-Irish dominated the populace. Their ways and customs differed greatly from the proper English mannerisms that Washington normally enjoyed in eastern Virginia. While living among them as a young surveyor, he described the Valley residents as "a parcel of Barbarian's and an uncouth set of People." Although a memorable quote, it reflected his first experiences among the frontier people several years before the war as a young scion from Tidewater Virginia aristocracy. One must wonder how much his opinions had changed over the last two years, as he had seen many of these types serving under his command and fighting bravely at Fort Necessity and on the Monongahela. Although they sought protection when confronted with a direct threat, few were willing to risks their lives or make sacrifices for the greater good of the region. The strong independent streak of the backcountry residents frustrated Washington as he attempted to organize the region's defenses. He grew irritated with their recalcitrance and told Dinwiddie, "In all things I meet with the greatest opposition. No orders are obeyed but what a party of soldiers or my own drawn sword enforces; without this not a single horse for the most urgent occasion cannot be had." He added that he would continue to enforce his orders when justified, "unless they execute what they threaten, i.e. to blow my brains out."[208]

Service in the Virginia Regiment proved as unpopular as ever. Washington informed Dinwiddie, "I greatly fear, we shall also proceed slowly in Recruiting." At Fredericksburg, the militia held a general muster, and the newly appointed company officers "began to express their apprehensions so soon as they had their Commissions." The militia refused to enlist, and the officers "were obliged to imprison the Men, who were afterwards Rescued by their Companions." At Winchester, Colonel George William Fairfax, colonel of the county militia, informed Dinwiddie that "at our general muster, we drafted pursuant to the Act made for that purpose 30 young men, out of which we could not get one to enlist, or pay the Ten pounds. Upon which we committed the whole to prison…and yesterday about twelve o'clock the prisoners artfully or by some assistance put the lock back, and took an opportunity of rushing out in a body with clubs, and through the guard, and have all made their escape."[209]

Washington directed Major Andrew Lewis to journey to Fredericksburg and organize new recruits for the expanded regiment. Washington soon headed out to Fort Cumberland, where he arrived on September 17. Having learned the hard lessons of campaigning in the Ohio Country, Washington created a "Scouts for Intelligence" unit, headed by the dependable frontiersman and his associate from 1753 and 1754 Captain Christopher Gist.

Washington reached Fort Cumberland on September 17, finding soldiers from several of the Virginia companies as well as Maryland and North Carolina men. He summoned the officers of the Virginia Regiment to a meeting that evening, bringing together the veterans and new men who were present. It was not long before Washington turned his thoughts to securing Indian allies. He sought the assistance of Andrew Montour again. Having funds available for his assignment this time, Washington apologized to Montour for his prior treatment, "tossed about from place to place and disappointed in your just expectations." Washington promised to rectify the inconveniences "as much as lies in my power."[210]

Washington did not linger at Fort Cumberland. He departed on about September 20, leaving Stephen in command with a list of ten items to take care of. They ranged from completing work on the fort to cleaning the barracks, cutting wood and other mundane duties. Washington requested Stephen "[t]o be particularly kind &c. to Captain Montour, and to treat the Indians, if any arrive with him, in the most familiar manner."[211]

Meanwhile, the situation on the Virginia frontier continued to deteriorate. After Braddock's defeat, French-aligned Indians attacked settlers in the Greenbriar Valley, killing twelve and carrying off eight women and children to the Ohio Country in August. After Washington finalized dispositions at Fort Cumberland, he headed off to August County, arriving in Staunton on

Photo of Emmanuel Episcopal Church in Cumberland, built atop the ramparts of Fort Cumberland, visible in the foreground. *Author photo.*

September 22. From there, he headed out to Fort Dinwiddie on the Jackson River, riding through Buffalo Gap and past Warm Springs. Washington arrived at the fort only a few days after its new commander, Captain Peter Hog, had relieved Andrew Lewis. Hog reported that the fort was in poor repair and that the settlers in the Greenbriar had abandoned their farms and "the best Crops of corn in the colony." Hog warned that unless troopers were sent to protect the area, Indians would take over the area and the harvest would be lost.

Washington ordered Hog to repair and strengthen the fort, emphasizing that he cut back the trees surrounding it so that it would not be within musket shot of the stronghold like Fort Necessity. He also instructed that they gather twelve months' worth of grain to keep the men fed and ensure that an adequate supply of beef was on hand. He did not delay at Fort Dinwiddie but rushed to Staunton by the next day before traveling to Alexandria and then Fredericksburg. Major Lewis informed him that only seventy recruits were at the latter place, with twenty-five gathered at Alexandria. George also received a message from Adam Stephen saying that Shawnees under French direction lurked about Fort Cumberland. They inflicted light casualties on

Adam Stephen's postwar home in the Shenandoah Valley, located in Martinsburg, West Virginia. *Author photo.*

the garrison and attacked local settlements. In response, Washington rushed a new company to reinforce Fort Cumberland.

Stephen described the situation there as "most deplorable." The attackers had cut off the garrison's communications with local inhabitants. Stephen explained that "barbarous circumstances, and unheard of instances of cruelty" had occurred. The attackers, he wrote, "spare the lives of the young women, and carry them away to gratify the brutal passions of the lawless savages."[212]

Ironically, the situation in late 1755 resembled the spring of 1754. Washington, now the colonel of the Virginia Regiment, remained behind with a detachment as Colonel Fry had done. Now Stephen commanded the forward elements at Fort Cumberland. Washington assembled the new companies as quickly as circumstances allowed and marched them from Fredericksburg to Winchester. He rode ahead and left Major Andrew Lewis to move the eighty-man detachment from Fredericksburg. The detachment marched out of town and crossed the Rappahannock River at the falls. It marched only seven miles, as Captain Charles Lewis reported that most of the troops were drunk. This circumstance also reflected poorly on the quality of the recruits. Thirty more recruits marched to Winchester from

Alexandria under Captain Thomas Waggener, joining twenty-two men of Captain David Bell's company. As Waggener's troops marched westward through the Blue Ridge, they encountered "crowds of people who were flying" eastward in fear of the Indians. Rumor had spread among them that Indians had torched Winchester. Washington sent messengers after the fleeing settlers "who are really frightened out of their sense" and lured them back to their settlements.[213]

On October 11, Washington wrote to Dinwiddie to fulfill his "indispensable duty to inform you particularly of my proceedings, and to give the most plain and authentic account from time to time of our situation." Washington's tone was changing from his frequent communications with Dinwiddie in 1754. Experience had tempered his emotions, and a more professional air emanated from his dispatches. Yet Washington found himself still dogged by his old nemesis of a British Regular army captain outranking a colonial colonel. This time it came in the form of Captain John Dagworthy, whose royal commission came from King George's War. In 1755, Captain Dagworthy arrived at Fort Cumberland by order of Maryland governor Sharpe. His presence placed him senior to both Washington and Stephen. Stephen wrote, "I have reason to believe Capt. Dagworthy will look upon himself as commanding officer after you have joined the troops," even though he only brought thirty men to the fort. The news affronted Washington's honor, and he consequently avoided the fort and made Winchester his headquarters.[214]

In early December, Captain Charles Lewis and Captain Robert Spotswood volunteered to accompany a detachment gathering corn from abandoned settlements. They arrived at Thomas Cresap's plantation on the Potomac River and "lodged this night in a comfortable house." The next day, Lewis and Spotswood hunted for deer. They later visited a house that had been "burnt by the savages." They discovered the body of a woman laying nearby, "her head being scalped, and also a small boy and a young man." "This horrid scene gave us a terrible shock," wrote Lewis, "but I hope with the leave of God, we shall still overcome the cruel, barbarous, and inhuman enemy." The horrid sights of service on the frontier only continued to worsen. Lewis recalled the scene: "We saw the bodies of three different people who were first massacred, then scalped, and after thrown into a fire. These bodies were not yet quite consumed but the flesh on many parts of them. We saw the clothes of these people yet bloody, and the stakes, the instruments of their death, still bloody, and their brains sticking on them, the orchards cut down, the mills destroyed, and waste of all manner of household goods." Lewis called this "the most horrid, shocking sight ever yet beheld."[215]

While the Virginians performed their duties around Fort Cumberland, Washington managed to find other localities to perform his duty and coincidentally avoid a showdown with Dagworthy. Recruiting and logistical problems provided him with apt reasons for his absence. He frequently took post in Alexandria, and Winchester in the Shenandoah was as close as he got to Fort Cumberland and Dagworthy. From these remote locales, he sent out communiques on the duller aspects of military command to Dinwiddie,

Opposite: Tunnels beneath Fort Cumberland (which remain under Emmanuel Episcopal Church) provided passage to soldiers and served as a storage area for food and ammunition. They were later used to assist escaping slaves as part of the Underground Railroad. *Author photo.*

This page: Washington's Office in Winchester, Virginia, where he spent much time avoiding Captain Dagworthy at Fort Cumberland and oversaw the design and construction of Fort Loudoun. *Author photo.*

Stephen and other officers and leaders. Through it all, the Dagworthy situation weighed heavily. Stephen and the officers of the Virginia Regiment made merry for Christmas at Fort Cumberland, drinking, singing and "and taking a cheerful glass." Meanwhile, George spent the day holed up in his headquarters at Winchester, a small building where he wrote orders for Captain Mercer to chase deserters.[216]

On December 28, Washington updated Stephen on the latest chatter from Dinwiddie on Dagworthy:

> *The Governor is very strongly of* [the] *opinion that Captain Dagworthy has no right to contend the command; and in his letter to me says…* "*but I am of opinion you might have obviated the inconsistent dispute with Captain Dagworthy, by asking him if he did not command a Provincial Company by virtue of Governor Sharpe's commission, as that* [commission] *he had formerly from his Majesty now ceases, as he is not on the half Pay list. If so, the method you are to take is very obvious, as your Commission from me is greater than what he has,*" *and in Williamsburg when I was down there, both he and Colo. Fitzhugh told me, that Dagworthy could have no more pretensions to Command me or either of the Field Officers of the Virginia Regiment than we have to command Genl Shirley—and further gave it as their opinions; that as Dagworthy's was only a botched up Commission at best.*[217]

Despite the strong language of support from Washington's Virginia patrons, he decided against confronting Dagworthy at Fort Cumberland. Instead, he remained in Winchester.

Washington complained to Dinwiddie, who elevated the issue to Governor Shirley of Massachusetts, the British North American commander. Dinwiddie requested him to rectify the situation, but no immediate remedy was provided. "I have impatiently expected to hear the result of your Honor's Letter to General Shirley," wrote Washington in early December, "and wish that the delays may not prove ominous. In that case, I shall not know how to act; for I can never submit to the command of Captain Dagworthy, since you have honored me with the command of the Virginia Regiment." Dinwiddie awaited an answer from Shirley, but a favorable resolution remained elusive. Shirley simply asked Governor Sharpe of Maryland to address the problem, so he informed Dagworthy that he commanded the fort but warned him not to give orders to the Virginians stationed there. Dagworthy disregarded Sharpe's orders and bragged that Sharpe directed him to command the

THE PEOPLE OF WINCHESTER APPEALING TO WASHINGTON

People of Winchester appeal to Washington. *Miriam and Ira D. Wallach Division of Art, Prints, and Photographs, New York Public Library Digital Collections.*

Virginians. This left Washington and Dinwiddie with the belief that Sharpe had ignored Shirley's orders.[218]

The situation continued into 1756, and the thought of serving under Dagworthy so rankled George that he once again pondered resignation. Instead, he took matters into his own hands and traveled to Boston to visit Shirley in person. He had met the man in Alexandria during the prelude to Braddock's campaign and been impressed with his bearing and dignity. Dinwiddie approved the journey skeptically, reminding George that the king chose officers to preside over his regiments. Washington ventured forth from Alexandria in early February 1756, accompanied by Captain George Mercer, Captain Robert Stewart and two hired servants, John Alton and Thomas Bishop. Washington's arrival at Philadelphia brought him to the largest city he had visited in his young life.

George spent several days in Philadelphia shopping for clothing and hats. On February 13, he departed, passing through Trenton, New Jersey, later the scene of his epic Revolutionary War victory over the Hessians. He arrived in New York on February 15. He connected with fellow Virginian

Beverly Robinson, brother of John Robinson, the Speaker of the Virginia House of Burgesses. Beverly had found success in New York, marrying the wealthy Susannah Philipse, whose twenty-six-year-old sister, Mary Eliza "Polly," resided with the Robinsons. Historians have speculated with some evidence that a love match may have developed between George and Polly while he visited the Robinson home in New York. Ultimately, nothing came from it, and she later married Roger Morris, Washington's comrade from Braddock's staff.

On February 20, he rode out of New York with his party headed for Boston, where he arrived on February 27. The *Boston Gazette* noted the arrival of "the Hon. Col. Washington, a gentleman who has deservedly a high reputation for military skill and valor, although success has not always attended his undertakings." He visited Governor Shirley at Province House, delivering Dinwiddie's correspondence. Dinwiddie reported on developments in Virginia and expounded on the Dagworthy episode. "He other ways acts in an arbitrary manner and insists on his rank superior to any of our offices, and he has not above 30 men, when Col. Washington has upwards of 500," lamented Dinwiddie.[219]

In the end, Shirley recognized Washington's superior rank over Dagworthy. He declared, "I do therefore give it as my opinion, that Captain Dagworthy, who now acts under a commission from the Governor of Maryland, and where there are no troops joined, can only take rank as a provincial Captain and of course is under the command of all field officers, and, in case it should happen, that Colonel Washington and Captain Dagworthy should join at Fort Cumberland, it is my order that Colonel Washington shall take the command."[220]

While George prevailed over Dagworthy, Shirley did not issue a British commission to Washington or take the Virginia Regiment into the British military establishment. On the return journey, George fell sick in Philadelphia, where he remained four days to recuperate. He stopped in Annapolis, Maryland, where he met Governor Sharpe. While Washington was en route to Williamsburg, he learned that Shirley also had assigned Governor Sharpe command of troops raised in the southern colonies. George believed that this undercut his authority and once again took the course of threatening to resign his commission. George's fears were unfounded, as Sharpe had directed Dagworthy not to interfere with the Virginia Regiment.[221]

Upon reaching Williamsburg, news of Indian raids into the frontier of Frederick and Hampshire Counties brought Washington to his senses. He

George Washington and Mary Eliza "Polly" Philipse, as portrayed by Howard Pyle.
Boston Public Library.

rushed back to Winchester, riding through Fredericksburg and crossing the Blue Ridge at Ashby's Gap. He found Winchester flooded with fearful settlers who had abandoned their homes on the frontier rather than risk attack at the hands of the Shawnees. He had only a small cadre of recruits from the Virginia Regiment to rely on and thus called out the militia, which as usual refused to muster in meaningful numbers. Washington later complained, "The timidity of the inhabitants of this Country, is to be equaled by nothing but their perverseness."[222]

Meanwhile, the raids continued to instill fear across the frontier, and Washington could do little to stem the violence. Delaware and Shawnee raiders under Bemino or John Killbuck raided settlements in the South Branch Valley and lured men from the frontier into a trap at the Battle of the Trough. Killbuck shortly struck again near Fort Edwards in the Battle of Great Cacapon. There, Killbuck enticed Captain John Mercer's Company of the Virginia Regiment into a trap and killed at least eighteen Virginians. It was frustrating time for Washington, and he could do little to effectively address the situation. When a frontiersman named Captain Robert Pearis and some Frederick County militia killed a French officer, coordinating the raids in a skirmish, Washington quickly grabbed credit, sending the Frenchman's scalp and the officer's orders from the French captain Daniel Dumas of Fort Duquesne to Lieutenant Governor Dinwiddie in Williamsburg.[223]

In May 1756, the Virginia House of Burgesses authorized Washington to begin construction of Fort Loudoun in Winchester, which started later that month. He detailed carpenters, masons and other workers from the Virginia Regiment to build the stronghold. Washington now utilized this construction as his latest reason to avoid Fort Cumberland. Historian Norm Baker described the fort: "It was a square fort built of horizontal timber and stone walls filled with earth and stone, with timber and stone bastions at each corner having flanks and faces of 25 feet and joined by curtains of 96 feet." One year after work began, the fort boasted sixteen cannons, but George hoped for more. The fortress made an impressive sight, situated atop an eminence on the northern outskirts of Winchester. Its defensive prowess, however, was never tested during the war, and it failed to prevent raids in the northern Shenandoah Valley. In 1757, the fort's guardhouse hosted several Cherokee Indians whom Washington reluctantly arrested for treason when directed by an Indian agent appointed by London. Washington warned against the arrests but was overruled. They were released in the end, but the affair damaged the alliance with the Cherokees.[224]

Washington was determined to have a well dug to supply water inside of Fort Loudoun in the event of a siege against Winchester. Over the course of three years, this well was dug and blasted with black powder to the depth of 103 feet. It still pumps water to this day. *Author photo.*

As spring turned to summer, seasonal Indian raids continued. The largest raid on the Virginia frontier struck southwestern Virginia near the Roanoke Valley. A large force of 205 Shawnee and Miami Indians from the Lower Ohio River and 25 French soldiers from the Great Lakes region struck. The raid killed 4 English soldiers and captured 22 prisoners. This raid caught Virginia off guard, as Washington had predicted that the attacks would focus on the northwestern frontier by the French and their allies operating from Fort Duquesne. Washington had miscalculated. Unable to quell the raids and lacking the resources to renew the offensive against Fort Duquesne, Washington settled on a chain of forts to protect the Virginia frontier. Yet this would be Washington's charge for the next two years until British authorities authorized the final move against Fort Duquesne in 1758.[225]

By the end of 1756, Washington had grown increasingly frustrated with his situation: "My strongest representation of matters relative to the peace of the frontiers are regarded as idle and frivolous; my propositions and measures as partial and selfish; and all my sincerest endeavors for

165

This cannon served as part of the armament of Fort Loudoun in Winchester. *Author photo.*

the service of my country perverted to the worse purpose. My orders are dark, doubtful, and uncertain; today approved, tomorrow condemned. Left to act and proceed at hazard, accountable for the consequence and blamed without the benefit of defense....However, I am determined to bear up under all the embarrassments some time longer, in hope of better

LORD LOUDOUN.

John Campbell, Earl of Loudoun,
British commander in North America,
1756–57. *Miriam and Ira D. Wallach
Division of Art, Prints, and Photographs,
New York Public Library Digital Collections.*

of regulation on the arrival of Lord Loudoun, to whom I look for the future fate of Virginia."[226]

Washington pleaded with Dinwiddie for leave to attend a conference that Loudoun had organized in Philadelphia with the governors. Dinwiddie doubted that Washington's presence would be of any use but permitted it "as you seem so earnest to go." While in Philadelphia, he learned that his journal from 1754 had been published by the French and was soon to be printed in English. This, of course, brought renewed attention to his actions at Jumonville Glen and Fort Necessity. While waiting for Loudoun, Washington had a translation made and "corrected as much of this as he could in the short time that remained before publication." Finally, Loudoun summoned Washington to meet on March 20 regarding forts on the Virginia frontier. George would be highly disappointed. Not only did Loudoun not elevate Washington and his command into the Regular Army, but his overall plan for 1757 also did not include a campaign to capture Fort Duquesne. Instead, Loudoun focused on New York and the North—and appropriately so. Contrary to Washington's desires, the North was where the war would be decided. Even more disheartening for George, Loudoun's plan transferred a significant detachment of the Virginia Regiment under Stephen to South Carolina for defensive purposes.[227]

The year 1757 did see Washington receive authority to issue punishments for desertion and other offenses against military discipline. He did not have to wait long to punish offenders from the Virginia Regiment. He constructed some gallows nearly forty feet high, and its mere existence terrified the men. "If I can be justified in the proceeding," he declared, "to hang two or three on it, as an example to others." He ordered two convicted deserters—Ignatious Edwards, who had committed the same offense on two prior occasions, and William Smith, "one of the greatest villains upon the continent"—to be hanged, although their sentence was death by firing squad. On July 28, 1757, he marched recently recruited companies and formed in front of the gallows at Winchester to witness the proceedings. Edwards and Smith were brought to the gallows and hanged for all to see. He later apologized to Dinwiddie: "Your honor will, I hope, excuse my hanging instead of shooting them. It conveyed much more terror to the others, and it was for example sake we did it."[228]

The year also saw the deterioration of Washington's relationship with Lieutenant Governor Dinwiddie, as the latter's health declined. Historian Jack Clary described Dinwiddie as growing "crabby" under the pressure of his duties and Washington as "impertinent." Washington remained thin-skinned to any criticism, real or perceived, and his correspondence does not reflect well on his professionalism and maturity. Dinwiddie's health and falling out of favor with Lord Loudoun soon forced his departure. As the year ended, Washington encountered his own health troubles, suffering another bout with "the bloody flux" accompanied by "bad fevers." However, Washington would have an opportunity with both a new governor and military commander in 1758.[229]

Chapter 11

"THE HAPPY ISSUE HE HAS BROUGHT OUR AFFAIRS"

Forbes's Campaign for Fort Duquesne

Lord John Ligonier, the commander in chief of British forces since September 1757, and Secretary of State William Pitt appointed acting brigadier general John Forbes to lead the 1758 effort against Fort Duquesne. Forbes came to this command an extremely sick man who was frequently incapacitated. Despite his ill health, Forbes planned to advance through Pennsylvania from Carlisle across the mountains to the Forks of the Ohio, delighting the Pennsylvanians. Virginians and Marylanders did not share the same enthusiasm for Forbes's chosen route. Colonel George Washington and the Virginians invested in the Ohio Company disagreed sharply with this plan. Washington knew the area well and truly believed it to be the better course of action with Braddock's Road already in place. Although Forbes had never visited the targeted region, he planned a campaign unlike any George had previously seen. Forbes implemented key supporting elements (military and diplomatic) that were just as important as the direct campaign itself. As for his new commander, Washington described Forbes as "a brave and good officer" who was "much debilitated by bad health."[230]

The British plans for 1758 were multifaceted. Pennsylvania had summoned the Ohio Country Indians to Easton, Pennsylvania, for peace negotiations. The objective was to remove them from their crucial role as allies to the French. Native support was critical to French success in the Ohio Country, but the Shawnees and Delawares had grown weary of the war and its impact on their communities. At the same time, the English planned an effort to capture Fort Frontenac where Lake Ontario emptied into the St.

Lawrence River, a vital link in the supply chain for Fort Duquesne and the French garrisons along the Allegheny north to Fort Presque Isle on Lake Erie. The British would also attack Fort Carillion near the southern area of Lake Champlain and make a second attempt to capture the French fortress at Louisburg on Cape Breton Island after failing in 1757. While success required patience, increased British coordination, manpower and resources would begin to wear the French down.

During the campaign, Washington's persistent lobbying for the usage of the Braddock's Road damaged his standing with Forbes and Sir John St. Clair, who had recovered from his Monongahela wounds and now served Forbes. Forbes lingered well to the rear for much of the summer, and his second-in-command Colonel Henry Bouquet, a skilled Swiss officer, coordinated the slow-moving advance across Pennsylvania. Bouquet initiated most orders and communications to Washington, coordinating closely with Forbes. The ailing general spent most of the summer issuing orders from the rear and organizing the peace conference with the Ohio Indians at Easton, Pennsylvania.

Bouquet had ordered detachments from the 1st Virginia Regiment to march from Fort Cumberland to Raystown, now Bedford, Pennsylvania. Major Andrew Lewis led the first 200 men, arriving on July 10. The Virginians arrived sporting hunting shirts and leggings that Washington had procured for them. Bouquet and Forbes thought highly of the garb and recognized its practicality in the wilderness campaign, so they made it the official "pattern of this expedition." Lieutenant Colonel Adam Stephen led another 335 Virginians to Raystown by July 12. The Virginians had served under Bouquet in Charlestown, South Carolina, in 1757 and had developed a rapport with him, appreciating the consideration that he displayed toward the provincial officers and troops. Meanwhile, Washington remained at Fort Cumberland, organizing and equipping Colonel William Byrd's Second Virginia Regiment. Although he was not with his regiments, Washington proudly wrote to Bouquet, "I may be allowed to say that from long intimacy and frequent scouting in these woods, my men are as well acquainted with all the passes and difficulties as any troops that will be employed, and therefore may answer any purpose intended by them, as well as any other body." When the Virginians arrived, Bouquet promptly put them to work building the new road.[231]

Meanwhile, a campaign of the political variety took some of Washington's attention in Winchester that summer. July 24, 1758, was an election day in Virginia. Colonel Washington had thrown his hat into the ring hoping

SITE OF
FORT CUMBERLAND
THE STORE HOUSES OF THE OHIO
COMPANY WERE FIRST LOCATED NEAR
THIS POINT. IN 1754 THE FIRST
FORT (CALLED MT. PLEASANT) WAS
BUILT. GEN'L. EDWARD BRADDOCK
ENLARGED THE FORT IN 1755 AND
RENAMED IT AFTER HIS FRIEND THE
DUKE OF CUMBERLAND.
STATE ROADS COMMISSION

Fort Cumberland
historic marker.
Author photo.

to gain a seat in the House of Burgesses representing Frederick County. He had requested leave for the event but decided against it out of concern that leaving his military duties during the critical military campaign would reflect poorly on his reputation. Washington lined up support from many of his established patrons, while George William Fairfax and John Carlyle used their influence to secure votes for Washington. He also invested heavily in the big event in Winchester in a fashion that was customary at the time. George funded the purchase of twenty-eight gallons of rum, thirty-four gallons of wine, forty-six gallons of beer, fifty gallons of rum punch and two gallons of cider to woo prospective voters on election day. The investment paid off, as the inebriated voters gave Washington the nod to represent them in Williamsburg. For now, however, the military campaign to capture Fort Duquesne remained his top priority, and he worked diligently to see that everything was done as he thought best to bring a successful conclusion. What George thought best did not always coincide with the plans of Forbes and Bouquet.

July 24 also proved to be an important date of decision in that campaign. Washington learned that Forbes had decided against Braddock's Road and determined to cut a new road over the mountains of Pennsylvania. The Virginia colonel could not abide by this decision, as his Virginia prejudices and sincere belief that Braddock's Road would be the best route blinded him to consideration of the other route. His correspondence with Bouquet over the matter, combined with his communications with Lieutenant Governor Francis Fauquier and other Virginians behind Forbes's and Bouquet's backs, reflects poorly on Washington's judgment. One would have thought that he would have moved passed the type of immature diatribes that marked his petty correspondence with Dinwiddie. However, his hubris and apparent willingness to undercut Forbes and Bouquet's decisions regarding the route revealed that his belief in the correctness of his opinions had outpaced his modesty and deference to senior officers.

Washington requested of Colonel Henry Bouquet, "Would it not facilitate the operations of the campaign if the Virginia troops were ordered to proceed as far/at least/as the Great Crossing of the Youghiogheny." He added, "Great advantages may certainly be derived." George was quick to add in a letter the next day that he would "cheerfully proceed to work on any road;—or pursue any route; or enter upon any service that the General or yourself can think me qualified for, or usefully employed in; and shall never have a will of my own where the point of duty is required at my hands."[232]

After reading Washington's letters, Bouquet informed Forbes that the Virginia colonel was "animated by a sincere zeal to contribute to the success of this expedition, and ready to march from whatever direction you may determine with the same eagerness." He added that Washington believed "that Braddock's Road is absolutely the only one to take." Bouquet and Washington met midway between Fort Cumberland and Raystown, Pennsylvania, at a settlement of a few houses. Bouquet reported to Forbes that he learned "nothing satisfactory." He added that Washington and his party "find everything easy which agrees with their ideas, jumping over all the difficulties." On August 2, Washington doubled down on using Braddock's Road in a lengthy diatribe outlining the advantages of Braddock's Road and the flaws with Forbes's proposed route. In the process, he damaged the goodwill he had earned with his previous offer to zealously adhere to whatever decisions were made. Four days later, he had to backtrack and reassure Bouquet, "The orders of any superior officer will, when once given, be law to me. I shall never hesitate in obeying them." He explained that until the direct order of the route was issued, he considered it "incumbent upon me to say what I could to divert you the commanding officer present from a resolution of opening a new road, of which I had the most unfavorable reports." While he agreed to adhere to orders, he added, "If I unfortunately am right; my conduct will acquit me of having discharged my duty on this important question." Washington, however, could not smooth things over with these professionals like he often did with Dinwiddie. Forbes accidentally learned of Washington's communications with Governor Fauquier regarding his meeting with Bouquet on the roads and informed Bouquet that he had uncovered George's scheme. Forbes declared, "A scheme that I think a shame for any officer to be concerned in." Forbes did not forget either, as on September 6 he requested Bouquet to consult with Washington but cautioned, "Although perhaps not follow his advice, as his behavior about the roads, was no ways like a soldier." Forbes continued in his doubts about Washington and noted that he had criticized Forbes's selected route without even having seen it.[233]

While the route was being worked out, Bouquet directed Washington to send large parties out on Braddock's Road for purposes of reconnoitering where a junction could be made with troops moving along Forbes's preferred route. In a letter of appreciation to Colonel James Wood of Winchester for his political support, Washington opined on the military situation: "I don't like to touch upon our Public Affairs; the Prospect is overspread by too many ill to give a favorable account. I will therefore say little—but yet say this, that backwardness appears in all things but the approach of Winter—that jogs on apace." To another he wrote, "Our Expedition seems overcast with too many ills to give you any satisfaction in a transient relation of them. God knows what's intended, for nothing seems ripe for Execution—backwardness, & I would (if dared) say more, appears in all things."[234]

After traveling from Fort Cumberland to Raystown to confer with Bouquet, Washington imprudently wrote to Francis Halkett, brigade major and son of the fallen Colonel Halkett of Monongahela fame. George declared, "If Colo. Bouquet succeeds in this point with the General—all is lost!—All is lost by Heavens!—our Enterprise Ruined; & We stopped at

General Braddock gifted Washington this pistol. He was "much exercised" by its temporary misplacement in 1777, "it being given him by Gen. Braddock, and having carried it through several campaigns, and he therefore values it very highly." *Smithsonian Museum of American History.*

the Laurel Hill for this Winter." Halkett had also served as Forbes's military secretary, and this correspondence "accidentally" ended up in the general's possession. Although Forbes remained seriously ill in Carlisle, he informed the British North American commander, Major General James Abercromby, of Washington's impudence. Forbes wrote, "I believe I have now got the better of the whole by letting them very roundly know, that their judging and determining my actions and intentions before that I had communicated my opinion to them was so premature and was taking the lead in so ridiculous a way that I could by no means suffer it."[235]

By August 20, Colonel James Burd and Major James Grant had departed Raystown with 1,500 troops to Loyalhanna, where they arrived in late August. There they constructed a storehouse and soon began entrenching the encampment that became Fort Ligonier. Located beyond the mountains, Ligonier served as the advanced outpost of supplies and the final staging area of Forbes's troops for the campaign against Fort Duquesne fifty miles away. Unlike Braddock, who attempted to carry his supplies via wagons the entire distance from Fort Cumberland to the forks of the Ohio, Forbes utilized a series of outposts along the way where supplies could be stored and the march broken up into smaller stretches. As for traversing the terrain between and Ligonier and Duquesne, Forbes explained to his commander that with the base at Loyalhanna, "at any time I can proceed to the Ohio, as all that country is mostly large nut and Oak wood without any brush below."[236]

As summer neared its close, the overall military situation brightened for the British. Although the French bloodily repelled General Abercromby's attack against Fort Carillion on July 8 in the last major French victory of the French and Indian War, the situation began to change quickly. Amherst and Admiral Boscawen captured the French stronghold of Louisburg. Lieutenant Colonel John Bradstreet with three thousand men captured Fort Frontenac by the end of August. The latter strained French supply routes to the Ohio Country and added to the pressure that the French were beginning to feel. On the diplomatic front, the Eastern branch of the Delaware Nation declared war against the French, a sign of deteriorating French and Indian alliances.

September 1 found Washington still encamped at Fort Cumberland feeling "very sickly and quite dispirited at the prospect before us." He complained to Speaker John Robinson, "That appearance of Glory once in view—that hope—those laudable ambitions of serving our country and meriting its applause is no more....In a word, all is lost." He went on to criticize Forbes

British howitzer at Fort Ligonier. *Author photo.*

British light twelve-pound cannon at Fort Ligonier. *Author photo.*

Fort Ligonier. *Author photo.*

and Bouquet behind their backs to fellow Virginians. "The conduct of our leaders (if not actuated by superior orders) is tempered with something I don't care to give a name to, indeed I will go further, and say they are d--s, to P-s-v-n artifice, to whose selfish views I attribute the miscarriage of this expedition, for nothing now but a miracle can bring this campaign to a happy issue." He believed that Forbes had wasted time building the new road and complained, "See therefore how our time has been misspent; behold the golden opportunity lost; and perhaps never regained." He even went so far as to propose informing the king "how grossly his honor and the public money have been prostituted." On a personal level, Washington maintained professional and cordial relations with his commanders and wished Forbes well in his recovery, which the general was "extremely obliged" to receive. Washington had also informed Forbes that Byrd had fallen ill, and the general, originally a doctor by education and training, expressed sorrow at hearing "my poor friend Colonel Byrd has been very bad" and wished Byrd could make it to Raystown, "where I should hope to prove a better physician than he will probably meet with at Fort Cumberland."[237]

Fortunately for Washington, Forbes never saw his letter to Robinson. He soon called Washington to Raystown to finalize their plans. Washington and Colonel Byrd traveled to Raystown, arriving on September 16. Adam Stephen traveled from Loyalhanna and informed Washington that it was impractical to build a road from Loyalhanna to Fort Duquesne. Washington brought this to Forbes's attention. Forbes promptly rebuked Washington and Byrd, explaining that no other officers who had seen both roads agreed with the Virginians' assessment. Forbes afterward wrote to Bouquet, "I told them plainly that whatever they thought…we had proceeded from the best intelligence that could be got for the good and convenience of the Army, without any views to oblige any one province over another." After going over the details of the plan, Forbes ordered Washington to return to Fort Cumberland the next morning and quickly march his remaining Virginians to Raystown. Washington complied, and Forbes welcomed him into the fold. Forbes called his officers together for a council of war and requested they submit plans for the final leg of the campaign. Washington dutifully drew up a plan based on his experience, and Forbes essentially adopted the strategy, boosting the Virginian's morale. Washington would play a leading role in the final advance.[238]

Washington's headquarters in Cumberland, Maryland. This cabin was originally within the fort but was later moved to its current location. Washington would have done much planning and complaining about the route the army was to use from this structure in 1758. *Author photo.*

Shortly before Washington arrived, the action had already heated up, albeit without authorization from Forbes. Bouquet detailed Major James Grant to take 400 Regulars from the British Royal American and Highlander regiments and 350 provincials on a reconnaissance to Fort Duquesne. The force included a large contingent of Virginians under the command of the experienced Major Andrew Lewis. When Bouquet and Grant informed Lewis of the plan, he objected due to the small size of Grant's force, lack of Indian support and the distance from Loyalhanna. They quickly overruled Lewis, but he insisted that his objections be noted. Awaiting them at Fort Duquesne were 500 French and Indians under the command of Captain François-Marie Le Marchand de Lignery. The French commander was no stranger to the Ohio Country and was awarded the Cross of St. Louis for his role in the French victory over Braddock on the Monongahela in 1755.[239]

Lewis's concerns proved valid, as the overly ambitious Grant pressed his luck and split his force in front of Fort Duquesne. Arriving in front of the fort on September 13, Grant ordered Lewis to lead four hundred men in a night attack against any forces he might find outside the fort. Grant waited, but no attack came. Lewis withdrew, explaining that the road was blocked with logs and the men were jittery moving in the darkness. The Virginian had prudently withdrawn, an action that angered Grant. On the next morning, Grant determined to attack, sending Lewis and his Virginians to guard baggage in rear, believing that he had failed in his duty the previous night. Grant sent a company of Highlanders toward the fort with drums beating and bagpipes playing to lure the French into an ambush by the main force situated atop a hill overlooking the fort. The French and Indians sallied out of the fort, quickly scattered the single company and then moved up the riverbanks to hit Grant on his flanks. It did not take long for the action to turn into a disastrous rout of Grant's force. He admitted, "I must own that I thought we had nothing to fear." Like Braddock in 1755, Grant did not want to leave the battlefield. "My heart is broke; I shall never out live this day!" With Grant's force collapsing, Lewis led most of his Virginians forward to save Grant and attempted to stop the French attack. However, the retreating Highlanders and Royal Americans made it nearly impossible for Lewis to succeed. Instead, his command took heavy losses, and he was captured. However, Captain Thomas Bullett's company had remained with the baggage, and his fifty Virginians vigorously attacked the French. His stand bought time for most of the survivors to escape. In the end, Grant lost more than 40 percent of his force in his ill-fated effort. Reports of Virginians' bravery circulated

Artistic rendition of the Battle of Grant's Hill, 1758, depicted at the Allegheny County Courthouse, Pittsburgh, Pennsylvania. *Author photo.*

back to General Forbes. He publicly praised Washington "on their good behavior." Washington proudly told his friend George William Fairfax that "every mouth resounds their praises." Captain Bullett in particular "acquired immortal honor in this engagement by his gallant behavior and long continuance in the field of action."[240]

Captain Lignery followed up his victory at Fort Duquesne with a raid against Fort Ligonier at Loyalhanna on October 12. He detailed more than 400 French troops and 150 western Delawares for the task. When musket fire erupted from the picket posts southwest of the fort, the acting commander, Colonel James Burd of Pennsylvania, sent 200 Marylanders to meet the threat, but the French quickly repelled them. Burd reinforced the Marylanders with the 1st Pennsylvania Battalion, but the French prevailed again, driving then back to the fort. The French and Indians pursued, but British artillery at the fort stopped their progress. The French force remained under cover, and when night came, it attempted another assault that the artillery repelled. Realizing the strength of Fort Ligonier, the French contented themselves with maintaining a sporadic musket fire, before carrying off two hundred horses and returning to Fort Duquesne. British losses tallied 12 killed, 18 wounded and 31 missing. The French reported the loss of 2 killed and 7 wounded.

Ironically, the several military engagements that occurred during Forbes's campaign played little role in its outcome. The decisive events played out elsewhere. First, Bradstreet captured Fort Frontenac on August 27, straining French supply lines to the Ohio Country. Closer to Forbes, the British finalized negotiations with the Iroquois, Shawnee and Delaware Indians, resulting in the Treaty of Easton on October 26. This treaty ended the Shawnee and Delaware alliance with the French. As these tribes had provided most of the manpower for French military actions in Pennsylvania, Maryland and Virginia, their removal from the war essentially crippled the ability of the French to operate and hold Fort Duquesne. Combined with supply difficulties, this led the French to ultimately scuttle and abandon that stronghold. Messengers raced to the Ohio Country to spread word of the treaty among the Native Americans, and Forbes remained patient, allowing time to word to reach the affected tribes to avoid confronting them in battle.

For the short term, Forbes's campaign continued. On November 12, French and Indian forces conducted a reconnaissance against Loyalhanna. Forbes dispatched Washington with the 1st Virginia Regiment and Lieutenant Colonel George Mercer commanding the 2nd Regiment to the front. Mercer confronted the French, while Washington attempted to surround them. The French slipped away in the enveloping darkness, and the two Virginia commands mistook each other for the enemy and opened fire. The friendly-fire incident killed one officer and thirteen men and wounded twenty-six others before Washington stopped it. He galloped "between two fires" with his drawn sword "knocking up" muskets and shouting for them to cease firing. After the American Revolution, he claimed that this was the most dangerous situation that he had ever been part of. However, Captain Thomas Bullitt, the hero of Grant's battle at Fort Duquesne in September, offered a differing perspective. He alleged that Washington did little to stop the incident and blamed him altogether for its occurrence. Forbes simply reported, "Unfortunately our parties fired upon each other in the dark."[241]

Amid this misfortune, there came a valuable piece of intelligence. Mercer had captured a French soldier who was an Englishman. Under threat of execution, he revealed to Forbes the sorry state of the French garrison at Fort Duquesne, as most of the troops had gone north for the winter and their Indian allies from distant lands headed home. Forbes determined to make an immediate march against Fort Duquesne and appointed Washington

Conestoga wagon at Fort Ligonier. *Author photo.*

as an acting brigadier in command of a brigade composed of the 1ˢᵗ and 2ⁿᵈ Virginia Regiments. Ironically, Washington, for all his complaints, found himself in the advance in charge of the road building. Even then, he communicated back to Forbes that if they should be "so fortunate" to capture Fort Duquesne, Braddock's Road was in better condition and would offer a better route of supply and communications from Fort Cumberland. Forbes's patience and multifaceted planning paid off on November 24, when reports of smoke rising from Fort Duquesne reached the British. The French abandoned the smoldering ruins of their fort, escaping via the Ohio River to Illinois. British forces entered the ruins of the fort the next day, and Washington's duty as he saw it was done: the Forks of the Ohio were in British hands. Forbes also performed the solemn duty of sending a burial party to Braddock's battlefield, where the skulls of 450 men were buried.[242]

For all of Washington's criticism of Forbes's conduct of the campaign, he readily acknowledged his efforts at its successful conclusion. To Lieutenant Governor Fauquier, Washington wrote, "Genl Forbes is very assiduous in getting these matters settled upon a solid basis; and has great merit (which I hope will be rewarded) for the happy issue he has brought our Affairs to—

British forces occupy the ruins of Fort Duquesne after the French burned and abandoned it, from a diorama at Fort Ligonier. *Author photo.*

infirm and worn down as he is." For all of George's griping and criticism of this campaign, Forbes's multifaceted approach to include negotiations with the French-allied Indians, his measured advance and persistence in the wake of Grant's disastrous defeat at Fort Duquesne achieved the desired outcome. Moreover, the Forbes campaign provided Washington a lesson in patience and perseverance that he later exhibited during the American Revolution. Ironically, he, like Forbes, would endure his share of upstarts and malcontents who thought that they knew better than Washington during the latter war.

Washington wasted no time returning to Virginia, reaching Winchester on December 8 with his Virginia soldiers. By December 20, he had returned to Mount Vernon and would never again leave it to participate in the French and Indian War, although it would be several years before it ended. He resigned his commission effective December 31, 1758, and departed military life to marry a wealthy woman with two children, Martha Custis. He returned and established a life for his new family at his beloved Mount Vernon on the Potomac. As for his military career, it would be another twenty-seven years before he donned his uniform and showed up in Philadelphia to assume command of the Continental army in 1775.

APPENDIX

This letter is from an unnamed officer in Washington's command at Jumonville. It was published on June 13, a short time after the action. Captain Adam Stephen wrote a letter shortly after the Battle of Fort Necessity in July that was likewise published in the Maryland Gazette. *He also wrote a letter published later in the year about Jumonville Glen. The second, later letter is more general in its nature and more conforming to the official after-action take. This author suspects that Stephen may be the author of this first letter and wrote the second letter to support Washington's account of the action at a time when he was being criticized over his actions in the Ohio Country.*

Maryland Gazette
June 13, 1754

We have a certain Account from the Westward of an Engagement between a party of English and French, on the 27th of May past, beyond the Allegany Mountains, in a place called The Flats, about 80 miles from our back settlements, about 240 miles N.W. of this place, and some miles to the Eastward of the new Fort on the Ohio, which was lately surrendered to the French by Capt. Trent. Some of the Particulars are as follows:

Major Washington had intelligence, from our friend the Half King, that a party of French were encamped on this side of the Fork, on which he immediately marched at the head of a company of about 40 men, but during their march the rains fell so heavy that they could scarce keep their ammunition dry; the French observed them before they came up, and speedily put themselves in order of battle, being under the command of Monsieur La Force. When the two parties approached nigh, the French (who were about 36 in number), gave the first fire, by which one of Major Washington's men was killed and another knock'd down. The English returned the fire, and killed 7 or 8 of the French, on which the rest took to their heels, but the Half King, and his Indians, who lay in ambush to cut them off in their retreat, fell upon them, and soon killed and scalped five of them. Monsieur Le Force finding that they were all likely to lose their lives under the hands of the savages, called to his men, and immediately, with great precipitation, ran towards the English, flung down their arms, and begged for quarter. Major Washington interposed between them and the Half King, and it was with great difficulty that he prevented the Indians from doing them further mischief, the Half King insisting on scalping them all, as it was their way of fighting, and he alleged that these people had killed, boiled and eat his Father, and that the Indians would not be satisfied without all their scalps; however, Major Washington at length persuaded him to be content with what scalps he had already got. One of the five killed and scalped by the Indians, was Monsieur Jumonville, an Ensign, whom the Half King himself dispatched with his tomahawk. Monsieur L Force and Twenty more Frenchmen, who were take prisoners, are carried down to Williamsburg. One or two, it is said, got away before the rest surrendered, and it is not known what has become of them. La Force has the character of an expert officer, and the Half King reckoned that the English had gained great advantage in taking him, telling Major Washington that that man (La Force) was [worth] *a thousand.*

NOTES

Introduction

1. Ward, *Breaking the Backcountry*, 28; Heyland, "Ohio Company, a Colonial Corporation," 6–7.
2. Delawares, Shawnees, Hurons, Potawatomis and Miamis were the principal tribes that inhabited this region and traded with the British. Iroquois people from the Seneca and Cayuga tribes, referred to as Mingos, had also filtered into the area. Ward, *Breaking the Backcountry*, 23; De Raymond to La Jonquiere, September 4, 1749, Collections of the Illinois Historical Library, 105–6.
3. The five original tribes of the Iroquois League consisted of the Mohawks, Oneidas, Onondagas, Cayugas and Senecas. The Tuscaroras later joined the nation. For an excellent discourse on the rise of the Iroquois and their domination of the Ohio Country, see Anderson, *Crucible of War*, 11–32.
4. Darlington, *Christopher Gist's Journals*, 29–30.
5. It should be noted that many of the tribes occupying the Ohio Country had been subjected to many schemes and outright frauds as English settlement spread inland from the coastal areas of North America. Additionally, the Iroquois had long delivered lands of vassal tribes to the British. One glaring example is the delivery of the Pennsylvania lands of the Delawares to the English at the Treaty of Lancaster. Anderson, *Crucible of War*, 18.
6. Brock, *Official Records of Robert Dinwiddie*, 17–18.

7. *Virginia Magazine of History and Biography* 13, "Treaty of Logg's Town, 1752," 154–74; Ward, *Breaking the Backcountry*, 28–29; Calloway, *Indian World of George Washington*, 54, 59.

8. Anderson, *Crucible of War*, 29.

9. Governor Robert Dinwiddie to the Board of Trade, October 6, 1752, and December 10, 1752, contained in Goodman, *Journal of Captain William Trent*, 69–75.

10. The English attempted to retain alliance with the Miamis but did not deliver promised gifts of powder and lead at conferences at Winchester, Virginia, and Carlisle, Pennsylvania. Langlade's raid on Pickawillany was planned well before the Logstown Conference, and the French could not have known of it then. Goodman, *Journal of Captain William Trent*, 32–34.

11. "Memorandum: Preliminary Conference with the Indians, 26 September 1753," Founders Online, National Archives, https://founders.archives. gov/documents/Franklin/01-05-02-0019.

12. King George II to Dinwiddie, August 28, 1753, U.K. National Archives, P.R.O., C.O. 5/211, 21–40, https://founders.archives.gov/documents/ Washington/02-01-02-0028#GEWN-02-01-02-0028-fn-0004.

13. McIlwane, *Journals of the House of Burgesses of Virginia*, xv–xvi, 103–4, 173; Message of Governor Dinwiddie to the House of Burgesses, contained in Brock, *Official Records of Robert Dinwiddie*, 39–40.

Chapter 1

14. Abbot, *Papers of George Washington*, 58, 60–61.

15. Stark, *Young Washington*, 5.

16. When Lawrence renamed the Little Hunting Creek plantation Mount Vernon, he did so in honor of Admiral Vernon.

17. Jackson, *Diaries of George Washington*, 1:10–11.

18. Ibid., 12.

19. Ibid., 13.

20. Ibid., 30.

21. Mount Vernon, https://www.mountvernon.org/george-washington/ washingtons-youth/journey-to-barbados.

22. Ibid.

23. Abbot, *Papers of George Washington*, 1:58.

24. Jackson, *Diaries of George Washington*, 130.

25. "Journey to the French Commandant: Narrative," Founders Online, National Archives, https://founders.archives.gov/documents/Washington/ 01-01-02-0003-0002.
26. Monacatoocha's formal Indian name was Scarouady, but he was known to the English as Monacatoocha or other slight variations of that name.
27. Darlington, *Christopher Gist's Journals*, 81.
28. Ibid.
29. Ibid. Also see Joseph L. Peyser's *Jacques Legardeur de Saint Pierre: Officer, Gentleman, Entrepreneur* for a detailed biography.
30. Jackson, *Diaries of George Washington*, 148–49.
31. Ibid., 151.
32. Darlington, *Christopher Gist's Journals*, 84–85.
33. Ibid., 86; Jackson, *Diaries of George Washington*, 155.
34. Ibid., 156.
35. Ibid., 158.

Chapter 2

36. Abbot, *Papers of George Washington*, 1:63. Original source is Dinwiddie to the Board of Trade, January 29, 1754.
37. While Dinwiddie hoped to scare the Indians with the fear of the French grabbing the Native American lands, Dinwiddie ultimately intended to settle the Ohio Country, which would displace the Indians. Brock, *Official Records of Robert Dinwiddie*, 55–57.
38. Brock, *Official Records of Robert Dinwiddie*, 52.
39. Dinwiddie also sent similar communications to Andrew Montour, a man of mixed Indian and French descent, who had established close relations with the Iroquois. Brock, *Official Records of Robert Dinwiddie*, 58.
40. Brock, *Official Records of Robert Dinwiddie*, 59.
41. Ibid., 53.
42. *Maryland Gazette*, March 14, 1754, in Abbot, *Papers of George Washington*, 67–68.
43. Brock, *Official Records of Robert Dinwiddie*, 1:93–98; Washington to Dinwiddie, March 9, 1754, in Abbot, *Papers of George Washington*, 73; Dinwiddie to Lord Fairfax, February 23, 1754, in Brock, *Official Records of Robert Dinwiddie*, 82.
44. Washington to Dinwiddie, March 7, 1754, in Abbot, *Papers of George Washington*, 71–72.

45. Dinwiddie to Holdernesse, March 12, 1754, in Brock, *Official Records of Robert Dinwiddie*, 93–98.

46. Dinwiddie to Washington, March 15, 1754, in Abbot, *Papers of George Washington*, 75–76.

47. Washington to Dinwiddie, March 20, 1754, and Washington to Richard Corbin, February–March 1754, in Abbot, *Papers of George Washington*, 78, 70.

Chapter 3

48. Jackson, *Diaries of George Washington*, 174–75; Anderson, *George Washington Remembers*, 16.

49. Abbot, *Papers of George Washington*, 82, 83.

50. Jackson, *Diaries of George Washington*, 177; Baker, *French and Indian War*, 6–7.

51. Ensign Edward Ward, Trent's second in command, gave two depositions. The first was on May 7, 1754, before Governor Dinwiddie and his council, and the second was given in 1756 and provided more details. The 1754 deposition was published with *Christopher's Gist's Journals* and focuses on events beginning on April 17. "Ensign Ward's Deposition (1756)," University of Pittsburgh, ULS Digital Collections.

52. "Ensign Ward's Deposition (1756)."

53. The storehouse on the Redstone became known as Redstone Old Fort. Ensign Edward Ward of Trent's company described it as "a strong square Log house with Loop Holes sufficient to have made a good Defence with a few men and very convenient for a Store House, where stores might be lodged in order to transported by water to the place where For Du Quesne now stands." "Letters from Messieurs Trent and Gist to Major Washington," *Maryland Gazette*, March 14, 1754; "Ensign Ward's Deposition (1756)."

54. "Ensign Ward's Deposition (1756)"; Darlington, *Christopher Gist's Journals*, 277.

55. Gallup, *Memoir of a French and Indian War Soldier*, 87–90.

56. The bateau was a most common vessel utilized on inland waterways in North America during the colonial period. A bateau measured thirty to forty feet in length and had a flat bottom. Darlington, *Christopher Gist's Journals*, 278.

57. Calloway, *Indian World of George Washington*, 62–63.

58. Ibid., 64.

59. "Ensign Ward's Deposition (1756)"; Darlington, *Christopher Gist's Journals*, 275–76.

60. Jackson, *Diaries of George Washington*, 178.

61. Abbot, *Papers of George Washington*, 65.

62. Fort Ohio is sometimes referred to as the New Store and was located on the site of Ridgely, West Virginia, on the south bank of the Potomac River across from Cumberland, Maryland. It was a blockhouse constructed by the Ohio Company primarily to store supplies. Ward noted that Trent had delayed his proposed return to the Forks with supplies to meet with Washington, who would soon be arriving at Fort Ohio. Regarding French numbers, Trent provided differing numbers. One thousand will be used here, as it is the figure that Trent supplied Washington. Jackson, *Diaries of George Washington*, 180.

63. The expected troops included 150 men of Fry's detachment from the Virginia Regiment, 300 North Carolinians, 100 Regulars from South Carolina and 150 Regulars from New York. The North Carolinians and New York troops did not arrive in time to participate, although Dinwiddie informed Washington that they were en route. Jackson, *Diaries of George Washington*, 180.

64. Ibid., 83–86.

65. Ibid., 88.

66. Ibid., 89.

67. Ibid., 94.

68. Ibid., 92.

69. Dinwiddie to Earl of Holderness, May 10, 1754, in Brock, *Official Records of Robert Dinwiddie*, 158.

70. Dinwiddie to the Lords of the Treasury, May 10, 1754, in Brock, *Official Records of Robert Dinwiddie*, 164.

71. Dinwiddie to the Lords for Trade, May 10, 1754, in Brock, *Official Records of Robert Dinwiddie*, 161.

72. Dinwiddie to Earl of Halifax, May 10, 1754, in Brock, *Official Records of Robert Dinwiddie*, 163.

73. Ibid., 91–93.

74. George Washington to Robert Dinwiddie, May 9, 1754, in Abbot, *Papers of George Washington*.

75. Stephen assumed that the French parties in the area were under the command of Jumonville, whom Washington would encounter in late May. Jumonville did not leave Fort Duquesne until May 23. Washington

to Dinwiddie, May 9, 1754, in Abbot, *Papers of George Washington*, 94–95; Stephen, "Ohio Expedition of 1754," 44–45; Jackson, *Diaries of George Washington*, 185–87.

76. Stephen, "Ohio Expedition of 1754," 45.

77. Jackson, *Diaries of George Washington*, 187.

78. Washington to Dinwiddie, May 18, 1754, in Abbot, *Papers of George Washington*, 95–96.

79. Abbot, *Papers of George Washington*, 98–99.

80. George Washington to Robert Dinwiddie, May 18, 1754, in Abbot, *Papers of George Washington*, 98–99.

81. Dinwiddie to Fry, May 25, 1754, in Brock, *Official Records of Robert Dinwiddie*, 170–71.

82. Turkey-Foot or Confluence is at the confluence of the Youghiogheny River, Casselman's River and Laurel Creek. Jackson, *Diaries of George Washington*, 190; Washington to Fry, in Abbot, *Papers of George Washington*, 101.

83. Washington to Fry, May 23, 1754, in Abbot, *Papers of George Washington*, 100.

84. Ibid., 101.

Chapter 4

85. Trudel and Kent, "Jumonville Affair," 351–81.

86. Peyser, *Ambush and Revenge*, 1–4; Russell, *Coulon de Villiers*, 33–43.

87. Trudel, *Introduction to New France*, 12–13; Account of Monceau contained in Contrecoeur to Marquis Duquesne, June 2, 1754, in Washington et al., *Memorial, Containing a Summary View of Facts, with Their Authorities*; Monsieur Druillon to Dinwiddie, June 1754, in Brock, *Official Records of Robert Dinwiddie*, 225; Affidavit Made Before His Excellency by John Shaw, August 27, 1754, in Harrington, *New Light on George Washington's Fort Necessity*.

88. Jackson, *Diaries of George Washington*, 191–93.

89. Ibid., 194.

90. Washington and his officers believed that La Force was the commander of the French force because of his prominence on the frontier.

91. Jackson, *Diaries of George Washington*, 294–95; Washington to Dinwiddie, May 29, 1754, in Abbot, *Papers of George Washington*; Adam Stephen, "Letter of Captain Adam Stephen of the Virginia Regiment," *Pennsylvania Gazette*, September 19, 1754.

92. Washington to Dinwiddie, May 29, 1754, in Abbot, *Papers of George Washington*, 110; Jackson, *Diaries of George Washington*, 195.

93. While Washington viewed the deployments as a joint effort, the fact that Indian warriors went in advance to scout French dispositions lends credence to the Half King and Monacatoocha taking the lead. "An Ohio Iroquois Warrior's Account of the Jumonville Affair, 1754," was located by historian David Preston in the UK National Archives, Colonial Office Papers. This citation is from Preston's book, *Braddock's Defeat*, 351–53; Washington to Dinwiddie, May 29, 1754, in Abbot, *Papers of George Washington*, 110; "Account from the Westward," *Maryland Gazette*, June 13, 1754. See appendix for this source in its entirety.

94. "Account from the Westward."

95. "Ohio Iroquois Warrior's Account," in Preston, *Braddock's Defeat*, 351–53.

96. George Washington to John A. Washington, May 31, 1754, in Abbot, *Papers of George Washington*; Stephen, "Letter of Captain Adam Stephen"; Freeman, *George Washington*, 423; Walpole, *Memoirs*, 346.

97. "Account from the Westward"; "Ohio Iroquois Warrior's Account," in Preston, *Braddock's Defeat*, 351–53; Anderson, *Crucible of War*, 53–54.

98. Anderson, *Crucible of War*, 53–54.

99. "Account from the Westward."

100. This quote has been widely attributed to British historian Horace Walpole, but evidence indicates that it did not originate with him. For further discussion, see https://boston1775.blogspot.com/2020/05/source-of-volley-fired-by-young.html.

101. Jackson, *Diaries of George Washington*, 196–98.

102. Ibid., 199.

103. Washington to Dinwiddie, May 29, 1754, in Abbot, *Papers of George Washington*, 107. See appendix on Jumonville for Washington's report to Dinwiddie.

104. Ibid. Dinwiddie to Fry, May 29, 1754; Dinwiddie to Muse, June 2, 1754, in Brock, *Official Records of Robert Dinwiddie*, 184–85, 187.

105. Washington to Dinwiddie, June 3, 1754, in Abbot, *Papers of George Washington*, 124.

Chapter 5

106. Ibid.

107. Jackson, *Diaries of George Washington*, 199, 209; Washington to Dinwiddie, May 29 and June 3, 1754, in Abbot, *Papers of George Washington*, 112, 124.

108. Dinwiddie to Washington, June 1, 1754, in Abbot, *Papers of George Washington*, 119.

109. Ibid.

110. Washington to Dinwiddie, in Abbot, *Papers of George Washington*, 123, 135.

111. Jackson, *Diaries of George Washington*, 199; Washington to Dinwiddie, in Abbot, *Papers of George Washington*, 123–24; Calloway, *Indian World of George Washington*, 91–92.

112. Dinwiddie to Innes, June 4, 1754, in Brock, *Official Records of Robert Dinwiddie*, 196.

113. A butt of wine is 108 gallons. Jackson, *Diaries of George Washington*, 199; Washington to Dinwiddie, in Abbot, *Papers of George Washington*, 123–24; Dictionary of Canadian Biography, "Stobo, Robert," http://www.biographi.ca/en/bio/stobo_robert_3E.html.

114. Jackson, *Diaries of George Washington*, 201.

115. Washington to Dinwiddie, June 10, 1754; John Carlyle to Washington, June 17, 1754, in Abbot, *Papers of George Washington*, 131, 140–41.

116. Dinwiddie to Washington, May 4, 1754, *Official Records of Robert Dinwiddie*, 148–49.

117. Washington to Dinwiddie, in Abbot, *Papers of George Washington*, 129–30.

118. Ibid., 137.

119. Ibid., 138.

120. Calloway, *Indian World of George Washington*, 92–93.

121. Letter from Captain Stephen, contained in the *Maryland Gazette*, August 29, 1754; account of Colonel James Wood, in Abbot, *Papers of George Washington*, 162.

122. "Minutes of a Council of War," June 28, 1754, in Abbot, *Papers of George Washington*, 155–56; Ibid., 162.

123. "Minutes of a Council of War," June 28, 1754, in Abbot, *Papers of George Washington*, 155–56; Deposition of John Shaw, August 27, 1754, in Harrington, *New Light on George Washington's Fort Necessity*, 68.

124. Deposition of John Shaw, August 27, 1754, in Harrington, *New Light on George Washington's Fort Necessity*, 68.

125. Calloway, *Indian World of George Washington*, 97–98.

Chapter 6

126. Contrecoeur to Duquesne, June 2, 1754, in Washington et al., *Memorial, Containing a Summary View of Facts, with Their Authorities*, 120–22.
127. The Native American contingent included warriors from Sioux of the Lakes, Huron, Abenaki, Iroquois of Fort de La Presentation, Nipissing, Algonquin and Ottawa tribes.
128. Peyser, *Ambush and Revenge*, 21–23; Russell, *Coulon de Villiers*, 47–68.
129. "Captain de Villiers Journal (Copy for Contrecoeur)," contained in Russell, *Coulon de Villiers*, 118–19.
130. Ibid., 119.
131. Ibid., 120–22.
132. Ibid., 123.
133. Ibid.
134. Ibid.

Chapter 7

135. Russell, *Coulon de Villiers*, 125–26; John Shaw deposition, in Harrington, *New Light on George Washington's Fort Necessity*, 68; Gallup, *Memoir of a French and Indian War Soldier*, 100.
136. Sources conflict on the exact timing of the discovery of the French. The 9:00 a.m. message from the Indians is important because it informed Washington of the size of the French force. He already knew that some enemy presence was in the area when, as Stephen reported, the first sentry was wounded and fired back. At least one other source does not mention the arrival of the French until 11:00 a.m. "Letter of Capt. [Adam] Stephen," *Maryland Gazette*, August 29, 1754; Stephen, "Ohio Expedition of 1754," 43–50; Harrington, *New Light on George Washington's Fort Necessity*, 68; Abbot, *Papers of George Washington*, 162.
137. Russell, *Coulon de Villiers*, 126.
138. Washington's presence with the regulars of the Independent Company of South Carolina is intriguing. It appears that Washington placed them in the vanguard, given their experience, and led them into battle. The tall Virginian took charge as the most serious challenge of his campaign, and he led from the front. Thus it would seem that while he had squabbles with Mackay over mundane affairs in camp and on the march, the two men worked together when the French appeared on the scene.

139. The French likely passed through some of the British camps and found these goods as they maneuvered. Russell, *Coulon de Villiers*, 126, 127; Greene, *Diary of Colonel Landon Carter*, 1:110–12.

140. Stephen, "Ohio Expedition of 1754," 43–50; John Shaw deposition, in Harrington, *New Light on George Washington's Fort Necessity*, 68.

141. "Account by George Washington and James Mackay of the Capitulation of Fort Necessity," Williamsburg, Virginia, July 19, 1753, in Abbot, *Papers of George Washington*, 160–61.

142. Abbot, *Papers of George Washington*, 160.

143. Some have speculated that the sound of drums was relayed to the French by a British-aligned Indian as a ruse. Russell, *Coulon de Villiers*, 127.

144. Anderson, *George Washington Remembers*, 17, 127.

145. In the joint Washington/Mackay after-action report, it is stated that Mr. Peyronee accompanied Van Braam to the talks with the French, as does the Shaw deposition. However, Peyronee was seriously wounded in the action. At least one historian has postulated that Peyronee was wounded after the parlay. If that had been the case, it would have been an unconscionable breach of the truce that existed. Such an incident would have certainly been noted by Washington, Mackay and others on the British side. All discussions of the impending surrender document focus on Van Braam and his limited ability with the French language and do not mention Peyronee. Furthermore, de Villiers mentions that they received only a single captain to the lines from the British. This author has concluded that the wounded Peyronee may have been involved in the initial discussions but was unable to continue, as the details of the agreement were hammered out by Van Braam, who was the clearly the interpreter at that point in the evening.

146. Russell, *Coulon de Villiers*, 127.

147. Original source cited contains both the French and English versions of the articles. It should be noted that the phrases in French referring to the assassination of Ensign Jumonville are *"de venger L'assasin qui a été fait sur un de nos officier"* in the preamble and *"l'assasinat du Sr de Jumonville"* in Article VII, in Abbot, *Papers of George Washington*, 165–68.

148. Mackay to Washington, August 27, 1754, in Abbot, *Papers of George Washington*, 194.

149. Gallup, *Memoir of a French and Indian War Soldier*, 102–4; Russell, *Coulon de Villiers*, 129–30; Shaw deposition, in Harrington, *New Light on George Washington's Fort Necessity*, 68.

150. Stark, *Young Washington*, 164; Harrington, *New Light on George Washington's Fort Necessity*, 69; Stephen, "Ohio Expedition of 1754," 50.

151. Gallup, *Memoir of a French and Indian War Soldier*, 102–4; Russell, *Coulon de Villiers*, 129–30.

152. Harrington, *New Light on George Washington's Fort Necessity*, 69; Anderson, *George Washington Remembers*, 18; William Fairfax to Washington, July 5, 1754, in Abbot, *Papers of George Washington*, 174; Alberts, *Charming Field for an Encounter*.

153. Peyser, *Ambush and Revenge*, 26; Russell, *Coulon de Villiers*, 60–61.

154. *Virginia Gazette*, July 19, 1754.

155. Dinwiddie to the Lords of Trade, July 24, 1754, in Brock, *Official Records of Robert Dinwiddie*, 241; Dinwiddie to Henry Fox, Secretary of War, July 24, in Brock, *Official Records of Robert Dinwiddie*, 245; Freeman, *George Washington*, 422.

156. Brock, *Official Records of Robert Dinwiddie*, 242.

157. Freeman, *George Washington*, 424.

158. Goldsbrow Banyar to William Johnson, July 23, 1754, and Johnson to Banyar, July 29, 1754, *Papers of Sir William Johnson*, 1:406, 409–10.

159. *Maryland Gazette*, August 29, 1754.

160. Preston, *Braddock's Defeat*.

161. *Maryland Gazette*, August 29, 1754.

162. Abbot, *Papers of George Washington*, 170–71.

163. Jackson, *Diaries of George Washington*, 172.

164. Sharpe to Washington, October 1, 1754, in Abbot, *Papers of George Washington*, 216; Washington to Stephen, July 20, 1776, in "From George Washington to Colonel Adam Stephen, 20 July 1776," Founders Online, National Archives.

Chapter 8

165. Dinwiddie wrote to the Lords of Trade in London and informed them of his plan for a renewed campaign against the French in the Ohio Country. Brock, *Official Records of Robert Dinwiddie*, 233–34, 248, 250, 261–62, 278–79; Dinwiddie to Washington, August 1, 1754, in Abbot, *Papers of George Washington*, 180–81.

166. Dinwiddie to Washington, August 3, 1754 (in response to Washington's unlocated letter of July 28), in Abbot, *Papers of George Washington*, 182.

167. Brock, *Official Records of Robert Dinwiddie*, 263, 264, 265.

168. Washington to William Fairfax, August 11, 1754, in Abbot, *Papers of George Washington*, 184.

169. Washington also wrote to Captain Mackay of the South Carolina Independent Company on August 15, but that letter remains unlocated. Innes to Washington, August 11, 1754, in Abbot, *Papers of George Washington*, 188, 189; Brock, *Official Records of Robert Dinwiddie*, 257.

170. Brock, *Official Records of Robert Dinwiddie*, 280.

171. Ibid., 287–88.

172. Ibid., 297, 308.

173. La Peronie to Washington, September 5, 1754, in Abbot, *Papers of George Washington*, 203–4.

174. Fitzhugh to Washington, November 4, 1754, and Washington to Fitzhugh, November 15, 1754, in Abbot, *Papers of George Washington*, 223–24, 225–26.

Chapter 9

175. This campaign has long been misunderstood, with many misperceptions being perpetrated over time regarding Braddock. For the definitive work, anchored in contemporary accounts, see Preston, *Braddock's Defeat*, 67.

176. Preston, *Braddock's Defeat*, 70–71; Robert Orme to George Washington, March 2, 1755, in Abbot, *Papers of George Washington*, 241.

177. Carlyle House Historic Park, "Carlyle House—History," Internet Archive, https://web.archive.org/web/20071214084241/http://www.nvrpa.org/parks/carlylehouse/?pg=braddock.html; Braddock to Robert Napier, April 19, 1755, in Pargellis, *Military Affairs in North America*, 84; Freeman, *George Washington*, 26.

178. The planned northern offensives of 1755 never came to fruition. Washington to William Fairfax, April 23, 1755, in Abbot, *Papers of George Washington*, 258.

179. Washington to William Fairfax, April 23, 1755, in Abbot, *Papers of George Washington*, 263–64. Washington to Mary Ball Washington, May 6, 1755, in Abbot, *Papers of George Washington*, 268; Freeman, *George Washington*, 2:28.

180. Freeman, *George Washington*, 3:32.

181. Washington's letter to Carlyle was never sent but revealed his thoughts on coming challenges for Braddock's campaign. Washington to Carlyle, May 14, 1755, in Abbot, *Papers of George Washington*, 274; George

Washington to John Auge Washington, May 14, 1755, in Abbot, *Papers of George Washington*, 277–78.

182. For a detailed account of the route and camps of Braddock's march, see Baker, *Braddock's Road*, 3:48.

183. In a June 14, 1755 letter to his brother, Washington also claimed credit for first suggesting that the army lighten its load by sending back the heavy wagons and artillery to Fort Cumberland. Preston, *Braddock's Defeat*, 181; Washington to Augustine Washington, June 28–July 2, 1755, in Abbot, *Papers of George Washington*, 320–21.

184. Washington to John Augustine Washington, June 28–July 2, 1755, in Abbot, *Papers of George Washington*, 319.

185. Roger Morris to Washington, June 23, 1755, in Abbot, *Papers of George Washington*, 315.

186. Anderson, *George Washington Remembers*, 19; Preston, *Braddock's Defeat*, 212–13.

187. Preston, *Braddock's Defeat*, 217–21; Sparks, *Writings of George Washington*, 2:469, Messner, *Reflections from Braddock's Battlefield*, 85.

188. "French Account of Beaujeu at the Monongahela," in Preston, *Braddock's Defeat*, 225, 355.

189. Preston, *Braddock's Defeat*, 222–23, 224, 355.

190. Ibid., 230.

191. Ibid., 237, 355, 356.

192. Washington to Mother, Washington to Dinwiddie, July 18, 1755, in Abbot, *Papers of George Washington*, 336–37, 339; Preston, *Braddock's Defeat*, 276.

193. Preston, *Braddock's Defeat*, 253.

194. Washington to Dinwiddie, July 18, 1754, in Abbot, *Papers of George Washington*, 340; Anderson, *George Washington Remembers*, 20, 21.

195. Anderson, *George Washington Remembers*, 20–21.

196. Washington to John Augustine Washington, July 18, 1755, in Abbot, *Papers of George Washington*, 343.

197. Preston, *Braddock's Defeat*, 270.

198. Anderson, *George Washington Remembers*, 21.

199. Ibid.

200. Dinwiddie to Innes, July 14, 1755, in Brock, *Official Records of Robert Dinwiddie*, 98.

201. Washington to Mother, Washington to Dinwiddie and Washington to John Augustine Washington, July 18, 1755, in Abbot, *Papers of George Washington*, 336–43.

202. Freeman, *George Washington*, 2:87; William Fairfax to Washington and Sally Fairfax, Ann Spearing and Elizabeth Dent to Washington, July 26, 1755, in Abbot, *Papers of George Washington*, 345–46; Washington to Robert Jackson, in Abbot, *Papers of George Washington*, 350.

Chapter 10

203. Dinwiddie to Washington, July 26, 1755, in Abbot, *Papers of George Washington*, 344.

204. George Washington to Augustine Washington, August 2, 1755, in Abbot, *Papers of George Washington*, 352.

205. Philip Ludwell to Washington, August 8, 1755; Charles Lewis to Washington, August 9, 1755; and Warner Lewis to Washington, August 9, 1755, in Abbot, *Papers of George Washington*, 355–59.

206. Washington to Mother, Washington to Warner Lewis, August 14, 1755, in Abbot, *Papers of George Washington*, 359–62.

207. "Appointment as Colonel of the Virginia Regiment," August 14, 1755, Founders Online, National Archives, https://founders.archives. gov/documents/Washington/02-02-02-0001-0002; Anderson, *George Washington Remembers*, 22; Freeman, *George Washington*, 2:112–13.

208. Hofstra, "A Parcel of Barbarians and an Uncooth Set of People," in *George Washington in the Virginia Backcountry*, 89; Washington to Richard, 1749–50, Washington to Dinwiddie, October 11, 1755, in Abbot, *Papers of George Washington*, 1:2:102.

209. Neill, *Fairfaxes of England and America*, 82.

210. Washington to Montour, September 19, 1755, Founders Online, National Archives, https://founders.archives.gov/documents/Washington/02-02-02-0048.

211. Washington to Stephen, September 20, 1755, Founders Online, National Archives, https://founders.archives.gov/documents/Washington/02-02-02-0050.

212. Stephen to Washington, October 4, 1755, Founders Online, National Archives, https://founders.archives.gov/documents/Washington/02-02-02-0068.

213. "Journal of Captain Charles Lewis"; Baker, *French and Indian War*, 24.

214. Stephen to Washington, October 4, 1755, Founders Online, National Archives, https://founders.archives.gov/documents/Washington/02-02-02-0068#GEWN-02-02-02-0068-fn-0006.

215. "Journal of Captain Charles Lewis," 215–16.

216. Stark, *Young Washington*, 294; Freeman, *George Washington*, 2.
217. Washington to Stephen, December 28, 1755, Founders Online, National Archives, https://founders.archives.gov/?q=washington%20 Period%3A%22Colonial%22%20Author%3A%22Washington%2C%20 George%22%20Recipient%3A%22Stephen%2C%20Adam%22&s =1111311113&r=9.
218. Freeman, *George Washington*, 2:154.
219. Ibid., 2:164; Dinwiddie to Shirley, January 24, 1756, in Brock, *Official Records of Robert Dinwiddie*, 4:328–31.
220. Freeman, *George Washington*, 2:166.
221. Clary, *George Washington's First War*, 192–93; Freeman, *George Washington*, 2:168.
222. Freeman, *George Washington*, 2:174.
223. Baker, *French and Indian War*, 42–43.
224. Ibid., 61; Norman Baker, "Fort Loudoun as Virginian's French & Indian War Command Center," French and Indian War Foundation, https://fiwf. org/fort-loudoun; Clary, *George Washington's First War*, 229.
225. The author is writing a second volume that will focus on Washington's efforts in the Shenandoah Valley and the Virginia frontier. Baker, *French and Indian War*, 63–64, 67.
226. Washington to John Robinson, December 19, 1756, as quoted in Freeman, *George Washington*, 2:231.
227. Freeman, *George Washington*, 2:237.
228. Ibid., 2:259.
229. Clary, *George Washington's First War*, 227.

Chapter 11

230. Anderson, *George Washington Remembers*, 22.
231. Freeman, *George Washington*, 2:316.
232. Washington to Bouquet, July 24, 1758, in Stevens, *Papers of Henry Bouquet*, 2:270.
233. Stevens, *Papers of Henry Bouquet*, 2:277, 278, 291, 298–301, 318–19, 344, 478, 536.
234. Washington to Colonel James Wood, July 1758, in Sparks, *Writings of George Washington*, vol. 2.
235. Washington to Francis Halkett, August 2, 1758, Founders Online, National Archives, https://founders.archives.gov/?q=%20

Author%3A%22Washington%2C%20George%22&s=1111311113&r=956&sr= ; Forbes to Abercromby, August 9, 1758, in James, *Writings of General John Forbes*, 173.

236. Forbes to Abercromby, August 11, 1758, in James, *Writings of General John Forbes*, 173.

237. The words are likely *dupes* and *Pennsylvanian*. Forbes to Washington, September 16, 1758, in Abbot, *Papers of George Washington*, 23–24; Washington to John Robinson, September 1, 1758, Founders Online, National Archives, https://founders.archives.gov/?q=john%20robinson%20Author%3A%22Washington%2C%20George%22&s=1111311113&r=68&sr=.

238. Stevens, *Papers of Henry Bouquet*, 2:277, 278, 291, 298–301, 318–19, 344, 478, 536.

239. Freeman, *George Washington*, 2:341–42.

240. Ibid., 2:345–46; Washington to G.W. and Sally C. Fairfax, September 25, 1757, in Abbot, *Papers of George Washington*, 39, 42.

241. Clary, *George Washington's First War*, 257; Abbot, *Papers of George Washington*, 6:122–23; McConnell, *To Risk It All*, 352.

242. Washington to Forbes, November 16, 1754, Founders Online, National Archives, https://founders.archives.gov/?q=washington%20to%20forbes%20Author%3A%22Washington%2C%20George%22%20Recipient%3A%22Forbes%2C%20John%22&s=1111311111&r=6; Clary, *George Washington's First War*, 258.

SELECT BIBLIOGRAPHY

Abbot, W.W., ed. *The Papers of George Washington: Colonial Series*. Charlottesville: University Press of Virginia, 1983.

Alberts, Robert C. *A Charming Field for an Encounter*. Washington, D.C.: National Park Service, 1975.

Anderson, Fred. *Crucible of War*. New York: Vintage Books, Division of Random House Inc., 2000.

———. *George Washington Remembers*. New York: Rowman & Littlefield Publishers Inc., 2004.

Ansyl, William H., Jr. *Frontier Forts Along the Potomac*. Parsons, WV: McLain Printing Company, 1984.

Axelrod, Alan. *Blooding at Great Meadows: Young George Washington and the Battle that Shaped the Man*. Philadelphia, PA: Running Press, 2007.

Baker, Norman L. *Braddock's Road: Mapping the British Expedition from Alexandria to the Monongahela*. Charleston, SC: The History Press, 2013.

———. *French and Indian War in Frederick County, Virginia*. Winchester, VA: Winchester-Frederick County Historical Society, 2000.

Brock, R.A. *The Official Records of Robert Dinwiddie, Lieutenant-Governor of the Colony of Virginia*. N.p., 1883.

Brown, Stuart E., Jr. *The Virginia Baron: The Story of Thomas, 6th Lord Fairfax*. Berryville, VA: Chesapeake Book Company, 1965.

Calloway, Colin G. *The Indian World of George Washington: The First President, the First Americans, and the Birth of the Nation*. New York: Oxford University Press, 2018.

Chartrand, Rene. *Monongahela 1754–55: Washington's Defeat, Braddock's Disaster*. Oxford, UK: Osprey Publishing, 2004.

Clary, David A. *George Washington's First War*. New York: Simon & Schuster, 2011.

Darlington, William M. *Christopher Gist's Journals with Historical, Geographical, and Ethnological Notes and Biographies of His Contemporaries*. Pittsburgh, PA: J.R. Weldin & Company, 1893.

Freeman, Douglas Southall. *George Washington: A Biography*. New York: Charles Scribner's Sons, 1948.

Galloway, Colin G. *The Indian World of George Washington*. Oxford, UK: Oxford University Press, 2018.

Gallup, Andrew, ed. *Memoir of a French and Indian War Soldier, "Jolicoeur," Charles Bonin*. Westminster, MD: Heritage Books, 2007.

Goodman, Alfred T., ed. *The Journal of Captain William Trent from Logstown to Pickawillany*. Cincinnati, OH: Robert Clarke and Company, 1871.

Greene, Jack P., ed. *The Diary of Colonel Landon Carter of Sabine Hall, 1752–1778*. 2 vols. Charlottesville: University Press of Virginia, 1965.

Harrington, J.C. *New Light on George Washington's Fort Necessity*. Fort Washington, PA: Eastern National Park and Monument Association, 1957.

Heyland, Herbert T. "The Ohio Company, a Colonial Corporation." *Quarterly Publication of the Historical and Philosophical Society of Ohio* 16, no. 1 (January–June 1921).

Hofstra, Warren R. *George Washington and the Virginia Backcountry*. Madison, WI: Madison House Publishers Inc., 1998.

Jackson, Donald, ed. *The Diaries of George Washington*. Charlottesville: University Press of Virginia, 1976.

James, Alfred Procter, ed. *Writings of General John Forbes*. Menasha, WI: Collegiate Press, 1938.

"Journal of Captain Charles Lewis of the Virginia Regiment, Commanded by Colonel George Washington in the Expedition Against the French, October 10–December 27, 1755." Collections of the Virginia Historical Society, 1892.

Koontz, Louis K. *The Virginia Frontier, 1754–1763*. Baltimore, MD: Johns Hopkins University Press, 1925.

Maass, John R. *George Washington's Virginia*. Charleston, SC: The History Press, 2017.

MacGregor, Doug. "The Shot Not Heard Around the World: Trent's Fort and the Opening of War for Empire." *Pennsylvania History: A Journal of Mid-Atlantic Studies* 74, no. 3 (2007): 354–73.

McConnell, Michael N. *To Risk It All: General Forbes and the Capture of Fort Duquesne*. Pittsburgh, PA: University of Pittsburgh Press, 2020.

McIlwane, H.R., ed. *Journals of the House of Burgesses of Virginia, 1752–1758*. Richmond: Virginia General Assembly, 1909.

Messner, Robert T. *Reflections from Braddock's Battlefield*. Braddock, PA: Braddock's Battlefield Association, 2005.

Murphy, R. Patrick. *The French and Indian War in Shenandoah County*. Basye, VA: Commercial Press Inc., 2013.

Neill, Edward D. *The Fairfaxes of England and America in the Seventeenth and Eighteenth Centuries, including Letters from and to Hon. William Fairfax…and His Sons, Col. George William Fairfax and Rev. Bryan, Eighth Lord Fairfax, the Neighbors and Friends to George Washington*. Albany, NY: J. Munsell, 1868.

O'Meara, Walter. *Guns at the Forks*. Pittsburgh, PA: University of Pittsburgh Press, 1979.

The Papers of Sir William Johnson. Vol. 1. Albany: University of the State of New York, 1921.

Pargellis, Stanley. *Military Affairs in North America, 1748–1765*. New York: D. Appleton—Century Company Inc., 1936.

Parkman, Francis. *Montcalm and Wolfe*. Boston: Little, Brown and Company, 1892.

Peyser, Joseph L. *Ambush and Revenge: George Washington's Adversaries in 1754*. Dunbar, PA: Stefano's Printing, 1999.

Preston, David. *Braddock's Defeat: The Battle of the Monongahela and the Road to Revolution*. New York: Oxford University Press, 2015.

Quarles, Garland R. *George Washington and Winchester, Virginia*. Winchester, VA: Winchester-Frederick County Historical Society, 1974.

Russell, Samuel, ed. *Coulon de Villiers: An Elite Military Family of New France*. Savanah, GA: Russell Martial Research, 2018.

Sargent, Winthrop, ed. *The History of an Expedition Against Fort Duquesne in 1755*. Philadelphia, PA: J.B. Lippincott & Company, 1856.

Sparks, Jared, ed. *The Writings of George Washington; Being His Correspondence, Addresses, Messages, and Other Papers, Official and Private, Selected and Published from the Original Manuscripts; with a Life of the Author, Notes and Illustrations*. Boston: Little, Brown and Company, 1855.

Stark, Peter. *Young Washington: How Wilderness and War Forged America's Founding Father*. New York: HarperCollins Publishers, 2018.

Stephen, Adam. "The Ohio Expedition of 1754." *Pennsylvania Magazine of History and Biography* 18, no. 1 (1894): 44–45.

Stevens, S.K., ed. *The Papers of Henry Bouquet*. Vol. 2, *The Forbes Expedition*. Harrisburg: Pennsylvania Historical and Museum Commission, 1951.

Tillberg, Fredrick. *Fort Necessity National Battlefield Site*. Harrisburg, PA: National Park Service, 1954.

Trudel, Marcel. *Introduction to New France*. Toronto: Holt, Rinehart and Winston of Canada, Limited, 1968.

Trudel, Marcel, and Donald H. Kent. "THE JUMONVILLE AFFAIR." *Pennsylvania History: A Journal of Mid-Atlantic Studies* 21, no. 4 (1954): 351–81.

Virginia Magazine of History and Biography 13. "The Treaty of Logg's Town, 1752" (1906): 154–74.

Walpole, Horace. *Memoirs of the Reign of King George the Second*. London: Henry Colburn, 1847.

Ward, Matthew C. *Breaking the Backcountry*. Pittsburgh, PA: University of Pittsburgh Press, 2003.

Washington, George, Jacob Nicolas Moreau, William Augustus Cumberland and Robert Napier. *A Memorial, Containing a Summary View of Facts, with Their Authorities: In Answer to the Observations Sent by the English Ministry to the Courts of Europe*. Philadelphia, PA: J. Chattin, 1757.

ABOUT THE AUTHOR

A lifelong student of military history, Scott C. Patchan's interest in George Washington and the French and Indian war was instilled as a child during summer visits to his grandparents' home in Uniontown, Pennsylvania, which often included a sojourn to nearby Fort Necessity National Battlefield. Walking those historic grounds and learning from the interpretive staff created the foundation for his interest in the study and preservation of America's historic sites. He grew up in Cleveland, Ohio, and graduated from James Madison University in the Shenandoah Valley of Virginia. He has published seven books with a heavy focus on the 1864 Shenandoah Valley Campaign of the U.S. Civil War and contributed dozens of essays and articles to numerous historical journals and publications. Each year, he conducts numerous historical tours and seminars on the colonial era, the Revolutionary War and the Civil War from New York to Georgia. He currently resides in the Wilderness area of Spotsylvania County, Virginia, and is active in preservation and interpretive efforts with the Shenandoah Valley Battlefield Foundation.

Visit us at
www.historypress.com